Grace's Sweet Life

Homemade Italian Desserts from Cannoli, Tiramisu and Panna Cotta to Torte, Pizzelle and Struffoli

Grace Massa Langlois

Ulysses Press

To Liana and Matthew, for your encouragement,
patience, and understanding...I love you!

• • •

Published by
Ulysses Press
P.O. Box 3440
Berkeley, CA 94703
www.ulyssespress.com

ISBN: 978-1-61243-024-9
Library of Congress Catalog Number 2011934781

Printed in the United States by Bang Printing

10 9 8 7 6 5 4 3 2 1

Acquisitions Editor: Keith Riegert
Managing Editor: Claire Chun
Editor: Lauren Harrison
Consulting Editor: Leslie Evans
Proofreader: Abigail Reser
Production: Judith Metzener
Design and layout: what!design @ whatweb.com
Photographs: © Liana Massa Langlois except page 200 © Cynthia Moore

Distributed by Publishers Group West

Contents

Note from the Author

It seems like only yesterday that I began sharing my desserts online. How could I know that my children, Liana and Matthew, would set me on a path that would awaken things in me that I thought were gone forever?

I'd spent years coming to terms with an injury that prevented me from returning to my career in business. Then when my husband passed away suddenly, I directed all my energy to my children. I needed to help them deal with the tragedy of losing their father. But one day Matthew was having a particularly bad day and in a burst of anger he shouted, "Mom, you don't understand! I didn't just lose my father. I lost you too!"

The awakening was surreal. I had to feel happy not only for my sake but also for theirs. So I turned to cooking, because making and sharing food provided me with so much comfort. I didn't see the change in myself, but my children did. The more I cooked, the happier I was. Then one day Liana and Matthew encouraged me to do something new with my love for food.

I can't pinpoint why I started blogging. But it soon became apparent that learning to blog not only kept my mind active and focused, but it also allowed me to enjoy cooking and sharing food. I repeatedly asked myself the same questions: What could I bring to the online food table? Would anyone find inspiration in what I had to offer? Would they share my passion for good food? But it all turned out so well. I never imagined that the joy I experience from cooking for the people I love would take me on one of the most exciting journeys of my life!

I am the second youngest of nine children. I grew up in Canada almost from birth, but you'd never know that if you walked into the red brick house I called home. My family has always been deeply rooted in the Italian culture and its traditions. That doesn't mean my parents didn't embrace North American culture, but I am so fortunate that they never left the Italian traditions behind.

The celebration of food has always been at the forefront of these traditions. Every special occasion was a blend of both cultures. At Thanksgiving, we enjoyed turkey with all the trimmings, but we started the meal with typical Italian fare: antipasto, *stracciatella* soup, homemade pasta with homemade sauce (often referred to as Sunday gravy), and usually a roast for good measure. We believed that food is for sharing, and there's always room at the table for a few more. We enjoyed the Italian meal between one and four o'clock, and then we came back to the table again at six for turkey, followed by espresso, coffee, and Italian sweets. At Easter, we children hunted and gathered treats that the Easter bunny had left for us. Meanwhile, my father was butchering lamb in the garage for the evening meal, and my mother could be found in the kitchen making the traditional *bombola* and *cavallo* (cookies shaped and decorated to look like dolls for girls and horses for boys), *celletti* (filled cookies; see page 103), and *fiadone* (sweet ricotta Italian-style cheesecake; see page 46). Christmas, my favorite holiday, was a two-day food affair. My parents were up at dawn, cleaning all the fish for the meal on Christmas Eve, later that day. The hustle and bustle in the house was like music to my ears. My older brothers and sisters would parade in to help with the preparations, like setting the table, rolling pasta, and making homemade sauce.

Growing up Italian, dessert was rarely eaten. It was generally served on special occasions, but most days, fruit was served for dessert. Our backyard was filled with grapevines and trees laden with peaches, apples, and pears. I remember that each meal was accompanied with fresh fruit, and my mother, on occasion, would serve baked apples in wine.

I recall a special ritual I shared with my papa when I was a little girl. Each night after supper, I would sit on his lap, and with paring knife in hand he would slowly cut two slices of fruit, one for me and one for him. Only after those two slices were enjoyed would he cut another two slices. Many years later the same feelings washed over me the first time I returned home from work to pick up my little girl. There was my papa with Liana on his lap. She was giggling, pulling at his ear, and poking his nose, and enjoying the same ritual that meant so much to me. Those same backyard apples were at the heart of our shared experiences.

When it comes to special celebrations like weddings and bridal showers, baking the coveted Italian cookie trays begins months in advance. Mothers, grandmothers, aunts, and friends of the family pull out their special family recipes before baking mountains of cookies. The night before the event all the bakers gather together and an assembly line kicks into motion. Big trays of cookies are built, then decorated with *cumbetti* (sugar-covered almonds) and chocolates. For bridal showers, each guest goes home with a plate piled high with every variety of cookie, as well as *cumbetti* and chocolates, and each plate is wrapped in cellophane and decorated with colorful ribbon.

When I look back on my childhood, it's hard for me not to associate food with happy memories. I recall coming home from school as a young girl and walking downstairs to my mother's makeshift kitchen in the laundry room. That's where she kneaded her bread and pasta dough, and where we canned bushels and bushels of tomatoes from the garden. This downstairs kitchen had a large wooden table that my father had made—perfect for making and rolling out dough. There were two other kitchens in the house as well. The main kitchen was primarily for everyday cooking, while the upstairs kitchen was reserved for baking cookies and bread. Even then, the only reason she used the upstairs kitchen was because she needed all three ovens.

Why three ovens? When my mother baked bread, she never made one or two loaves, but sixty! I still marvel at the fact that this woman could knead dough by hand for sixty loaves much more easily than I can knead one loaf. Imagine the almost intoxicating aroma of sixty baking loaves wafting throughout the house, out the windows and into our neighborhood. I prayed that I would be the first one to arrive home from school so I could claim the ends of the crusty bread. I'd cut into the hot loaf and a puff of steam would escape. Spreading Nutella on homemade bread just out of the oven was sheer heaven.

When my mother made *cicerchiata* (Italian honey balls; see page 144), it reminded me of homemade gnocchi (potato dumplings), except that the balls were much smaller. She always let me join in, and my job was rolling out the *cicerchiata* dough into long ropes. She told me that when she was a young girl, they made *cicerchiata* with leftover scraps of pasta dough. I looked forward to when she fried the tiny balls that resembled chickpeas, because I knew soon they would be drenched in sweet honey.

Looking back I realize why I have such a passion for making and sharing food. When my mother was teaching me how to roll pasta or make cookies I didn't just learn the art of cooking and baking. The precious time spent together gave my mother the opportunity to share stories about life, traditions, and the importance of family. With each lesson in the kitchen, I learned the qualities that make me the person I am today: Waiting for the dough to rise taught me patience. Bringing new flavors together taught adventure. Knowing that we eat with our eyes first taught creativity. Watching people enjoy my freshly prepared treats taught fulfillment. And most important, tasting the freshest ingredients taught me to appreciate the best things in life.

I thank my mother for these lessons learned years ago. And I thank my children for setting me on this enriching journey of sharing my love of food with the world. With the recipes in this book, I pass on to you, my reader, those same traditions and virtues I gained from growing up surrounded by the love, generosity, and bountiful spirit of an Italian family kitchen. *Entri come amici, vada come familgia* (Enter as friends, leave as family).

Buon appetito!

NOTES ON MEASUREMENTS

Measurements of ingredients in this book are listed by both weight (grams, milliliters, ounces) and volume (cups, teaspoons, tablespoons). Because baking requires precision, weighing your ingredients is preferred, and using a good digital kitchen scale will ensure your ingredients are accurately measured.

Cream varieties in this book are not listed by milk-fat percentage, but in general, these are the percentages I use: half-and half (10%); light cream, also sold as coffee cream or table cream (18 to 30%; I use 18%); and heavy cream, also sold as whipping cream (33 to 35%; I use 35%).

NOTES ON SPECIAL INGREDIENTS

Liquid glucose is a type of invert sugar. Invert sugar is ideal for baking because it helps to prevent crystallization. It's often used in professional kitchens because it provides a smooth mouthfeel in preparations like sorbet, gelato, ice cream, ganache, fudge, and especially caramel. It also helps to improve flavor and texture, increases tenderness and moistness, and also helps to preserve baked goods. It can be difficult to find, but I've been able to locate it at my local bulk food store and online. Wilton (www.wilton.com) also packages liquid glucose, and their products are available at Michael's Arts & Craft stores (www.michaels.com). If you're not able to find a jar, corn syrup is a good substitute.

Lievito vaniglinato or *lievito per dolci*, often referred to as "yeast for cake," is a type of baking powder flavored with vanilla. It's very popular in Italian baking and helps give baked goods a good rise and a delicious flavor. It would seem that the simplest substitution would be adding vanilla and baking powder to a recipe, but it isn't so easy. The Italian baking powder *lievito vaniglinato* is a single-acting baking powder, while North American is a double-acting baking powder. Therefore, the two products are not interchangeable.

Lievito vaniglinato used to be difficult to find, but is now readily available at Italian grocers, specialty markets, and online. One small package (about 6½ teaspoons or 16 g) raises 4 cups (500 g) of flour. Popular name brands are Bertolini and Paneangeli. Another brand to look for is Dr. Oetker; if you are able to locate this brand, keep in mind it is not flavored with vanilla. Adding one or two teaspoons of vanilla extract to your recipe will provide that beautiful flavor.

Vanillina aroma per dolci (vanilla flavoring for sweets) is a powder popular in Italian baking to flavor cakes creams, coulis/compotes, ice cream, and sauces, and it's also used in many chocolate applications. It's available in 0.5-gram packets at Italian grocers and also online. Popular brands are Paneangeli and Bertolini.

Doppio zero or "00" flour is highly refined, powder-soft wheat flour milled in Italy. It can be found at Italian grocers or online. It's often substituted with all-purpose flour, but if you can find the real thing, I urge you to try it because it is wonderful in a variety of baked goods, and also can be used for making pasta dough and pizza dough. It's best to find a product that is directly imported from Italy.

Gelatin is available in two forms, powdered or sheet (also referred to as leaf). Unfortunately, it's very difficult to convert between the two because you can't use a straight substitution based on weight. Gelatin is graded by "bloom," which measures the strength of the gelatin. The strength of powdered gelatin is different from sheet gelatin, but please note that sheet gelatin is available in different strengths (often labeled silver, gold, or platinum). To complicate matters, the strength can also vary from one brand to another. It's best to stick to one brand because, with use, you will become familiar with the amounts that work best. When in doubt, refer to the package instructions.

The popular powdered gelatin brand is Knox. Each box contains 4 packages of about 2¼ to 2½ teaspoons (7 grams), which sets 2 cups (500 ml) liquid. I stock both types of gelatins in my pantry, but I find sheet gelatin easier to work with because it dissolves better than the powdered gelatin. In Canada where I live, the most popular brand of sheet gelatin is Dr. Oetker. The strength is gold extra. Each package contains 6 sheets weighing a total of 10 grams and it sets 2 cups (500 ml) of liquid.

Basics

Crema Pasticcera

MAKES ABOUT 3 CUPS

Pastry Cream

Crema pasticcera can be made several ways. The basic recipe consists of milk, egg yolks, sugar, flavorings, and flour or cornstarch, which act as thickeners. The many variations to the basic recipe include replacing the milk with a combination of milk and cream, which makes the pastry cream richer. Additional egg yolks will yield a richer cream. For a dessert in which the pastry cream is the star of the show or needs to be more stable so it can hold a shape, I usually use these variations to prepare a richer pastry cream, as in the Torta Millefoglie (page 86). You may prefer lighter pastry cream for filling éclairs (page 149) or doughnuts (page 151). Flavor variations for pastry cream are endless: steep the dairy with cinnamon, espresso beans or powder, or shredded coconut. Add extracts, chocolate or nut pastes. With a little imagination you can take a simple dessert and turn it into something extraordinary.

> 2 cups plus 2 tablespoons (500 ml) whole milk
>
> 1 vanilla bean, split and seeded
>
> 6 large egg yolks, at room temperature
>
> ⅔ cup plus 1 tablespoon (160 g) superfine sugar
>
> ⅓ cup (40 g) all-purpose flour, sifted

1. Reserve ½ cup (120 ml) milk. In a small saucepan over medium heat, bring the remaining milk and the vanilla bean and seeds just to a boil. Remove from the heat, cover, and allow vanilla to steep for 10 to 12 minutes.

2. In a medium bowl using a large whisk, beat the egg yolks and sugar until pale in color, 3 to 4 minutes.

3. Add the flour and continue to whisk until smooth. Gradually add the reserved milk and whisk to combine well.

4. Gradually pour the egg mixture into the vanilla-infused milk whisking to combine well.

5. Cook over medium heat, whisking constantly until thickened, 3 to 5 minutes.

6. Strain the custard through a fine-mesh sieve into a small heatproof bowl (discard the solids).

7. Place a sheet of plastic wrap directly onto the surface of the custard to prevent a skin from forming as it cools. Refrigerate until ready to use.

Crema Pasticcera al Cioccolato Bianco
White Chocolate Pastry Cream

Follow the basic Crema Pasticcera procedure with the following modifications:

1. Reduce the whole milk to 2 cups (475 ml).

2. Reduce the sugar to ⅔ cup (150 g).

3. Increase the flour to ¼ cup plus 2 tablespoons (47 g).

4. In Step 5, remove from the heat and whisk in 4 ounces (113 g) finely chopped white chocolate until the custard is smooth, then proceed with Steps 6 and 7.

VARIATION *Crema Pasticcera al Cioccolato*
Chocolate Pastry Cream

Follow the basic Crema Pasticcera procedure with the following modifications:

1. Decrease the sugar to ½ cup plus 2½ tablespoons (125 g).

2. In Step 5, remove from the heat and whisk in 4 ounces (113 g) finely chopped good-quality semisweet or bittersweet chocolate until the custard is smooth, then proceed with Steps 6 and 7.

VARIATION *Crema Pasticcera 2*
Pastry Cream 2

Follow the basic Crema Pasticcera procedure with the following modifications:

1. Reduce the whole milk to 1 cup plus 1 tablespoon (250 ml).

2. In Step 1, add 1 cup plus 1 tablespoon (250 ml) heavy cream to the pan with the milk and the vanilla.

3. Increase the egg yolks to 7 large egg yolks total.

Crema Chantilly

Chantilly Cream

Crema chantilly is very delicate. For best results, prevent the loss of volume by whipping the chantilly cream just prior to using or by storing in an airtight container in the refrigerator for no longer than 3 hours before using. For the best flavor, combine the cream and the vanilla bean and seeds in an airtight container, then cover and refrigerate for 24 hours. If you do not have time to allow the vanilla bean to infuse in the cream, substitute 1½ teaspoons pure vanilla extract. For best results, chill the mixer bowl and whip attachment (or bowl and beaters or balloon whisk) for 30 minutes prior to whipping the cream. If you're whipping the cream on a warm day, while beating, set the bowl in an ice water bath to keep it cold.

> 2 cups plus 2 tablespoons (500 ml) heavy cream
>
> 1 vanilla bean, split and seeded
>
> ¼ cup (31 g) confectioners' sugar

1. Combine the cream and the vanilla bean and seeds in an airtight container. Stir to combine. Cover and refrigerate for 1 hour, or preferably 24 hours, to allow the vanilla to infuse.

2. At least 30 minutes before whipping the cream, put the bowl and whip attachment of a stand mixer in the freezer. Just prior to whipping, remove the vanilla cream from the refrigerator and strain through a fine-mesh sieve into the cold bowl (discard the solids).

3. Fit the mixer with the whip attachment and begin beating the cream at high speed (to immediately incorporate air) until soft peaks (curl when attachment is lifted) form, about 2 minutes. Reduce the speed to low and gradually add the confectioners' sugar. Increase the speed to high and continue beating to stiff peaks (stand up straight when attachment is lifted), about 2 minutes longer.

4. If not using immediately, transfer to an airtight container and refrigerator until ready to use, no longer than 3 hours.

Panna Montata Zuccherata

Sweetened Whipped Cream

As freshly whipped cream deflates quickly, it's best to whip it just before serving. Serve with macerated fruit, dollop onto spoon desserts like panna cotta, baked custard and mousse, or use to garnish tarts.

> *1 cup (240 ml) heavy cream*
>
> *2 tablespoons (16 g) confectioners' sugar, sifted*
>
> *½ teaspoon pure vanilla extract*

1. Chill a large bowl, a large balloon whisk, or the beaters of a handheld mixer, and the cream.

2. Place the cream, confectioners' sugar, and vanilla in the cold bowl. Using the cold whisk or beaters at high speed, whip the cream until you've reached your desired consistency. For soft peaks, whip the cream until the peaks are rounded or curl when the beaters are lifted. For stiff peaks, whip the cream until peaks stand up straight when the beaters are lifted.

3. If not serving immediately, transfer the whipped cream to an airtight container and refrigerate for up to 3 hours before using.

VARIATION **Panna Montata al Cacao**
Sweetened Whipped Cream with Cocoa

Follow the basic Sweetened Whipped Cream procedure with the following modifications:

1. Increase the confectioners' sugar to 3 tablespoons (24 g).

2. Add 1 tablespoon unsweetened cocoa (not Dutch process), sifted, when you add the confectioners' sugar.

TIME-SAVING TIP FOR SWEETENED WHIPPED CREAM

I very rarely purchase ready-made whipped cream anymore. I prefer to purchase cream in 1-liter cartons with resealable lids. When I return home from the market, I split two vanilla beans in half, scrape out the seeds, and place both the seeds and the beans in the carton. I seal the lid, give the carton a good shake, and store it in the refrigerator. In the morning when I'm reaching for the coffee cream, I give the carton a shake. When I need whipped cream, I pull out the carton and whip the amount I need. It's cold, convenient, and, best of all, fresh and flavorful. The infused cream can also be used in a number of different preparations like custards, cakes, and ganache.

Crema di Ricotta

Ricotta Cream

This filling can be made one day in advance and refrigerated in an airtight container. *Crema di ricotta* is the filling used in the coveted *Cannoli Siciliani* (page 137) but it is very versatile. Use it as a filling for rolled brandy snaps, sandwich cookies, zeppole, cupcakes (page 77), tarts, *millefoglie* (page 86) or *pizzelle* cups (page 93). If using to fill tarts or *pizzelle* cups, garnish with fresh fruit or berry compote. Omit the chocolate chips and candied citrus and fold in 1 to 1½ cups whipped cream for a lighter version perfect for serving over macerated berries or crumbles.

> 3 cups (660 g) fresh ricotta, drained overnight
>
> 1⅓ to 1½ cups (167 g to 188 g) confectioners' sugar, sifted
>
> 1½ teaspoons pure vanilla extract
>
> ⅓ cup (50 g) finely diced candied citron or candied orange peel, or a combination (optional)
>
> ⅓ cup (80 g) miniature semisweet chocolate chips

1. Place the drained ricotta in a stand mixer fitted with the paddle attachment. Beat on medium speed until smooth, 2 to 3 minutes.

2. Add 1⅓ cups (167 g) confectioners' sugar and the vanilla. Beat until fluffy and very smooth, about 4 minutes. Taste, add the remaining confectioners' sugar as needed, and beat until smooth.

3. Stir in the candied citrus, if using, and the chocolate chips.

4. Transfer to an airtight container and refrigerate until ready to use.

Meringa all'Italiana

Italian Meringue

Meringue is an egg foam made with a combination of egg whites and sugar. There are three types of meringue: Swiss, French, and Italian. For French meringue, superfine sugar is gradually beaten into egg whites. For Swiss meringue, the egg whites and sugar are whisked together over simmering water, then beaten to stiff peaks and baked. Italian meringue uses boiled sugar syrup, which produces a stable meringue that can be used in many pastries without collapsing. It makes a light and fluffy frosting and can be used as a base for semifreddo and macarons.

> ¾ cup plus 2 tablespoons (200 g) superfine sugar
>
> ⅓ cup (80 ml) water
>
> 3 large egg whites, at room temperature

1. In a small saucepan over medium heat, stir the sugar and water until the sugar dissolves, then stop stirring; stirring after the sugar dissolves could cause crystalization and ruin the meringue. When the syrup is clear, attach a candy thermometer to the saucepan. When the syrup has almost reached a temperature of 240°F (116°C), remove from the heat and immediately detach the thermometer. (The syrup will continue to cook off the heat and reach the correct temperature quickly; pulling the saucepan off the heat a couple of degrees sooner will prevent going over the ideal temperature.)

2. Meanwhile, as the sugar syrup reaches a temperature of 230°F (110°C), in a stand mixer fitted with whip attachment, begin beating the egg whites at low speed until foamy. Increase the speed to medium and continue beating to soft peaks.

3. When the syrup comes off the heat, reduce the mixer speed to low, and with the mixer running, gradually add the sugar syrup to the egg whites, pouring the syrup in a steady, thin stream down the side of the bowl; do not let the syrup touch the beaters. Increase the speed to high and beat until cool, about 85°F (29°C), the egg whites form stiff peaks, and the meringue is thick and glossy.

TIPS FOR SUCCESSFUL MERINGUE

- Separate the egg whites from the yolks directly upon removing them from the refrigerator. Eggs are much easier to separate when cold. Be sure the egg whites are completely yolk free.

- Before you begin whipping the egg whites, let them come to room temperature to ensure the greatest volume.

- Use the correct type of bowl. A copper bowl is best, but if one is not available, use a stainless steel or glass bowl that has been rinsed with vinegar, which will ensure the bowl is ultraclean and free of grease.

- For Italian meringue, cook the sugar syrup until it reaches 230°F to 250°F (110°C to 120°C). The temperature of the sugar syrup determines the texture of the meringue; the higher the temperature, the firmer the texture will be. If you don't have a thermometer, fill a small bowl with very cold water and drop a bit of sugar syrup in; if it forms a soft ball, the syrup is at the proper temperature.

- When adding the sugar syrup to the egg whites, be sure to keep the syrup away from the beaters, or the beaters will splash the syrup along the sides of the bowl rather than incorporating it all into the egg whites.

Pasta a Bomba

Egg Foam Base for Semifreddo and Mousse

Pasta a bomba is an egg foam base made with a combination of egg yolks and cooked sugar syrup that is whipped to a creamy consistency. It is very similar to an Italian meringue, but it uses the egg yolks rather than the whites. *Pasta a bomba* is a base component used in a number of different dessert recipes: French buttercream, mousses, parfaits, ice cream bomb, and semifreddo. It can be stored for up to two days in the refrigerator (before using, beat to soften) or up to two months in the freezer (thaw for 15 minutes and beat lightly to soften).

⅓ cup (80 ml) water

¾ cup plus 2 teaspoons (180 g) superfine sugar

6 large egg yolks, at room temperature

1. In a small saucepan over medium heat, stir the water and sugar together until the sugar dissolves, then stop stirring (to prevent crystallization). When the water is clear, attach a candy thermometer to the saucepan. Continue to cook the sugar over medium heat.

2. Meanwhile, in a stand mixer fitted with the paddle attachment, beat the egg yolks at high speed until fluffy and pale in color.

3. When the sugar syrup almost reaches 243°F (117°C), immediately remove from the heat and detach the thermometer.

4. Reduce the mixer speed to low and, with the mixer running, gradually add the sugar syrup to the egg yolks, pouring the syrup in a steady, thin stream down the side of the bowl onto the yolks (to prevent splashing, make sure the syrup doesn't touch the paddle attachment). Increase the mixer speed to high and beat until the mixture thickens and cools to about 85°F (29°C), 3 to 5 minutes.

Pasta Frolla 1

Sweet Pastry Dough 1

Pasta frolla is a classic Italian pastry dough used in almost all of Italy's sweet pies and tarts. The dough is also used in a number of traditional cookies. It's tender, rich, and sweet with a crumbly texture when baked. The Italian word *frolla* translates in English to "crumbly." It's quick and easy to prepare either by hand, food processor, or stand mixer. It's usually made with butter but can also be made with vegetable oil (if making the dough with oil, it's not necessary to chill the ingredients, and it requires only a 15 minute resting period at room temperature). It's often flavored with lemon zest, orange zest, or vanilla (seeds or pure vanilla extract). There are nut variations and also chocolate variations. *Pasta frolla* can be stored wrapped in plastic in the refrigerator for up to 1 week, or well wrapped in plastic and then sealed in a freezer bag or airtight container in the freezer for up to 1 month.

> 2 cups (250 g) all-purpose flour
>
> ⅓ cup (75 g) superfine sugar
>
> pinch of salt
>
> freshly grated zest of ½ lemon
>
> ½ cup plus 1 tablespoon (125 g) cold unsalted butter, cut into ¼-inch cubes
>
> 2 large egg yolks
>
> 1 teaspoon pure vanilla extract, or seeds from 1 vanilla bean
>
> 1 to 2 tablespoons (15 to 30 ml) ice water, as needed

1. In a food processor, pulse together the flour, sugar, salt, and lemon zest (vanilla seeds if using) until combined.

2. Add the butter and pulse about 8 times until the mixture resembles coarse meal.

3. In a small bowl, lightly beat together the egg yolks and vanilla with a fork.

4. With the food processor running, gradually add the egg mixture through the feed tube. Process just until the dough starts to come together (do not overprocess). Test the dough by squeezing a small amount together with your fingers. If the dough is crumbly, add the ice water 1 tablespoon at a time, pulsing just until the dough starts to come together.

5. Transfer the dough to a lightly floured work surface; divide the dough according to the recipe directions. Lightly knead each portion into a ball. Flatten each ball into a disk, and wrap tightly in plastic. Refrigerate the disks for at least 1 hour prior to rolling.

Chocolate Sweet Pastry Dough

Follow the procedure for Sweet Pastry Dough 1 with the following modifications:

1. Increase the flour to 2⅓ cups plus 1 tablespoon (300 g).

2. Add ⅓ cup (40 g) unsweetened cocoa powder (not Dutch process) to the flour mixture.

3. Replace the superfine sugar with 1 cup (130 g) confectioners' sugar.

4. Omit the lemon zest.

5. Increase the cold unsalted butter to ⅔ cup plus 1 tablespoon (160 g).

6. Increase the large egg yolks to 3.

VARIATION *Pasta Frolla alle Nocciole*   MAKES DOUGH FOR 2 (8-INCH) CRUSTS
Hazelnut Sweet Pastry Dough

Follow the procedure for Sweet Pastry Dough 1 with the following modifications:

1. Add ⅓ cup (50 g) toasted hazelnuts, finely ground (see page 20), and ¼ teaspoon cinnamon to the flour mixture.

2. Increase the sugar to ⅓ cup plus 1 teaspoon (80 g).

3. Omit the lemon zest.

4. Increase the butter to ½ cup plus 2 tablespoons (140 g).

5. Replace the egg yolks with 1 large whole egg plus 1 large egg yolk, lightly beaten with a fork.

6. Omit the vanilla.

TIPS FOR MAKING PASTA FROLLA

- Begin with very cold butter. I chill all the ingredients, besides the eggs, in the freezer for at least 30 minutes.

- Be sure to combine the ingredients quickly, otherwise the dough will develop too much gluten, making it difficult to work with and causing the pastry to toughen when baked.

- I prefer to prepare the dough with a food processor. It keeps my warm hands off the dough and it takes only a few minutes to come together.

- If you prefer to prepare the dough by hand and if you find the dough warming at any point, place the dough back in the refrigerator for 10 to 15 minutes.

- Make sure the dough rests in the refrigerator for at least 30 minutes prior to rolling and cutting the pastry. Otherwise, again, the pastry will be difficult to work with.

Pasta Frolla 2

Sweet Pastry Dough 2

This *pasta frolla* is made with vegetable oil, and it's the type of pastry dough my mother has been making since she was a young girl. In fact, I don't believe she's ever made *frolla* with butter. It's a recipe that's been handed down from generation to generation. When I asked her, "Mom, why don't you use butter?" she was rather quick with her response: "We couldn't afford butter, and even if we could, the availability of butter was rare." My mother grew up during the war, and butter was scarce; on the occasion it was available, it was far too expensive. At that time, sweet treats in general were a rarity and often enjoyed only around Christmas or Easter if at all. Over the years, she never felt the need to adjust the recipe to include butter because everyone enjoyed it as is. It's the pastry she uses in her *fiadone dolce di ricotta* (sweet ricotta cheesecake), a family favorite. I for one am happy she didn't adjust the recipe because it's easy to make, the dough is very forgiving, and it's delicious.

This recipe calls for *lievito vaniglinato* (yeast for cake with vanilla), However, I have found success in this recipe by substituting the *lievito* with 1 teaspoon of baking powder and 1 teaspoon of pure vanilla extract or the seeds from 1 vanilla bean.

> 3¾ cups plus 2½ teaspoons (475 g) all-purpose flour, divided
>
> 3 large eggs, at room temperature
>
> ⅓ cup (80 ml) vegetable oil
>
> ¾ cup plus 4 teaspoons (185 g) granulated sugar
>
> ½ cup (120 ml) whole milk
>
> 1 package (½ ounce or 16 g) lievito vaniglinato (see page 8)

1. Using a fine-mesh sieve, sift the flour into a medium bowl. Set aside.

2. In a stand mixer fitted with the paddle attachment, beat the eggs and the oil on high speed for 1 minute.

3. Reduce the speed to low, and with the mixer running, gradually add the sugar. Increase the speed to medium and beat to combine, about 1 minute.

4. In a small bowl, use a fork to stir together the milk and *lievito vaniglinato* until the *lievito* is dissolved. Immediately, with the mixer running at low speed, add the milk mixture to the egg mixture. Work quickly because the *lievito* will bubble up. Beat to just combine.

5. Decrease the mixer speed to low, and, with the mixer running, gradually add 2 cups (250 g) of the flour. The dough should start to come together at this point. Remove the bowl from the stand mixer and stir in the remaining flour with a wooden spoon.

6. Turn the dough out onto a lightly floured work surface and gently knead until smooth, about 3 minutes.

7. Divide the dough in half. Form each piece into a ball, and gently press each ball into a disk. Cover with a kitchen towel and let the dough rest at room temperature for 15 minutes before rolling.

Pasta Brisè per Crostate
Pie Dough

MAKES DOUGH FOR 2 (10-INCH) CRUSTS

> 2½ cups (313 g) all-purpose flour
>
> 1 teaspoon salt
>
> 1 tablespoon superfine sugar
>
> ¾ cup (170 g) unsalted butter, cut into ½-inch cubes
>
> 4 to 6 tablespoons cold water

1. Place all of the ingredients in the freezer to chill for 30 minutes.

2. In a food processor, process the flour, salt, and sugar until well combined.

3. Add the cold butter and process until the mixture resembles a coarse crumb, about 15 seconds.

4. With the processor running, drizzle 2 tablespoons ice water through the feed tube and process for 30 seconds. Repeat with another 2 tablespoons water. Test the dough by squeezing a small amount together between your fingertips; it should hold together without being wet or sticky. If the dough is crumbly, add more ice water 1 tablespoon at a time.

5. Divide the dough in half. Form each piece into a ball and flatten each ball into a disk, wrap in plastic, and refrigerate for 1 hour. (If not using immediately, the dough can be stored, well wrapped, in the freezer for up to 1 month.)

SKINNING AND TOASTING NUTS

Blanching almonds: Place the almonds in a heatproof bowl and cover with boiling water. Let stand for 2 minutes. Drain through a colander and run coldwater over the almonds. Slip the skins off with your fingers and pat the nuts dry with a kitchen towel. Store in an airtight container in the refrigerator or freezer.

Toasting and steaming hazelnuts, pistachios and walnuts: Preheat the oven to 350°F (180°C). Arrange the nuts in a single layer on a rimmed baking sheet and bake until golden, 8 to 10 minutes. Wrap the warm nuts tightly in a kitchen towel and set aside to steam for 5 minutes. Rub the nuts together in the towel to remove the skins. Toasting is not necessary if you use this method.

Toasting nuts in a skillet: Preheat a skillet over medium heat and add the nuts in a single later. Toast until golden, stirring frequently, 6 to 8 minutes. Transfer to a heatproof dish to cool completely.

Toasting nuts in the oven: Preheat the oven to 350°F (180°C). Arrange the nuts in a single layer on a rimmed baking sheet and bake until golden, 8 to 10 minutes. Transfer to a heatproof dish to cool completely.

Pralinata di Nocciola

Hazelnut Praline

Praline is a very versatile candy. It can be processed to a crumb (fine or coarse) and used to garnish mousse, ice cream, panna cotta, or a number of other sweet treats. It can also be processed to a paste and used in desserts like Torta Sette Strati (Seven-Layer Cake, page 57). The praline can also be broken into shards and used as a decoration, again for a number of different desserts, like Tartellette al Cioccolato e Caramello con Nocciole (Chocolate, Caramel, and Hazelnut Tartlets, page 123). The hazelnuts can be substituted with other nuts, like almonds, pine nuts, or walnuts, or you can also use a combination. I really enjoy pairing hazelnuts and almonds for praline.

When processing the hazelnuts into a crumb, process only the amount you'll need and store the remaining larger pieces wrapped in parchment paper and closed in a resealable plastic bag or airtight container in the freezer for up to one month. Store hazelnut praline paste in an airtight container in the refrigerator for up to one month or several months in the freezer.

> 1⅔ cups (250 g) hazelnuts, toasted, skinned, and cooled (see page 20)
>
> 1 cup (225 g) superfine sugar
>
> 2 tablespoons (25 g) glucose (see note)
>
> ⅓ cup (80 ml) water

1. Line a rimmed baking sheet with parchment paper and lightly coat with vegetable spray, or use a silicone baking mat. Place an 8-inch ring mold (or the ring of an 8-inch springform pan) on the lined baking sheet. Place the hazelnuts in the mold in a single layer. Lift the mold up off the baking sheet.

2. In a medium nonstick saucepan over medium heat, bring the sugar, glucose, and water to a boil over medium heat, stirring until the sugar and glucose have dissolved. Continue to cook the syrup, without stirring, to a light amber color, about 320°F (160°C), occasionally swirling the pan over the heat and brushing down the sides of pan with a pastry brush dipped in water.

3. Pour the sugar syrup directly over the hazelnuts, making sure all the hazelnuts are evenly coated. Set aside to cool, allowing the praline to set, about 1 hour.

4. To process the praline into a paste, break the praline into small pieces. Transfer the praline pieces to a food processor and process to a thick smooth paste. (Depending on the size of your food processor you may want to process praline in 2 or 3 batches. Be patient through the process because it can take some time to obtain a smooth paste, 5 to 10 minutes.) Transfer the paste to an airtight container and refrigerate until ready to use.

5. To process the praline into crumbs, break the praline into small pieces, transfer to a food processor, and pulse to fine or coarse crumbs. Or if you prefer, break praline into medium pieces and transfer to a resealable plastic bag. Using a rolling pin, crush to fine or coarse crumbs.

Note: I like to use a combination of glucose and superfine sugar because the glucose helps prevent crystallization while the sugar cooks, but if you don't have any on hand, increase the sugar by 2 tablespoons (25 g).

Pasta Sfolgia

Puff Pastry

Making *pasta sfoglia*, or puff pastry, can be a challenge. Its relatively few ingredients must be carefully prepared to achieve the light dough that grows into so many flaky buttery layers in the oven. The preparation for *pasta sfoglia* is very similar to that of *pâte feuilletée* (puff pastry), but the folding process is slightly different and the number of "turns," or folds, can vary. Traditionally, *pasta sfoglia* dough is folded in fourths, rather than in thirds like *pâte feuilletée*. I prepared this *pasta sfoglia* using five turns and a combination of two folding methods, the single fold (letter fold) and the double fold (book fold). Making homemade puff pastry may seem daunting at first, but by understanding a few basic terms and the process, it gets easier with a little practice. And the reward for perfecting this heavenly pastry is that it opens you up to a world of sweet pastries like *cannoncini* (custard-filled pastry horns), *millefolgie* (the Italian version of mille-feuille), *ventaglietti* (palmiers), and *sfolgiatelle* (shell-shaped cream-filled pastries).

To store *pasta sfoglia*, wrap the pastry in parchment paper first, then in plastic, and then in an airtight container. It can be kept in the refrigerator for up to five days, or frozen for three to four weeks (always make sure to thaw the pastry in the refrigerator before rolling it out). If I plan on freezing the dough, I generally make only four turns and do the fifth after it has thawed. For convenience, I generally make a double recipe. I use one half immediately and freeze the other half for later use.

> 2 cups (1 pound, 454 g) very cold unsalted butter
>
> 3½ cups plus 1 tablespoon (454 g) 00 (*doppio zero*) flour (see page 8), or 2½ cups (313 g) all-purpose flour plus 1¼ cups (125 g) cake flour
>
> 1 teaspoon salt
>
> 1¼ cups (300 ml) cold water

uno TO PREPARE THE *PANETTO* (BUTTER BLOCK)

1. Working quickly, place the sticks of butter side by side on a sheet of parchment paper. (If you are using one full-pound piece of butter, cut it in half lengthwise and set the two pieces side by side on the parchment paper.) Cover the butter with a second sheet of parchment paper. Using a rolling pin, pat down and roll out the butter into a rectangle about ¾ to 1 inch thick. Wrap the butter in plastic wrap and refrigerate until cold and firm, about 30 minutes.

due TO PREPARE THE *PASTELLO* (BASE DOUGH)

1. Using a fine-mesh sieve, sift the flour onto a clean work surface or into a large bowl and make a well in the center of the flour. (If using a combination of all-purpose flour and cake flour, sift into a large bowl and then whisk together to combine well before making the well.) Dissolve the salt in the water. Pour ¾ cup (180 ml) of the salted water into the well and use your fingers to gradually draw the flour into the water. Gradually add the remaining salted water while drawing in more flour with your fingers. Work the flour and water together with your fingers to make the dough. Form the dough into a rough ball. Do not knead the dough; it should be rough and sticky. Using the tip of a sharp

paring knife, slash a cross pattern (about ½ inch deep) into the surface of the dough (to help relax the gluten in the dough). Wrap the dough with a damp kitchen towel or plastic and refrigerate for 15 to 30 minutes.

tre TO PREPARE THE *PACHETTO* (DOUGH PACKAGE)

1. Remove the base dough from the refrigerator and unwrap. Transfer the dough to a clean, lightly floured work surface. Flatten the dough with your hands. Using a lightly floured rolling pin, roll out each arm of the cross, creating a slightly raised center (this will act as a bed for the butter block, so make sure the bed is large enough). Use a pastry brush to brush away any excess flour on the surface of the dough. Remove the butter block from the refrigerator, unwrap, and place the butter block on the raised center of the dough. Fold one arm of dough over the butter block and then fold the opposite arm over. Repeat with the two remaining arms, making sure the butter block is completely encased. (Stretch the dough if necessary to ensure the butter block is completely enclosed.) Seal the edges by pinching the dough together with your fingertips. (If the butter has softened, use a pastry brush to brush off any excess flour, wrap the dough package in plastic, and refrigerate for 15 minutes.)

2. If needed, lightly flour the work surface and the surface of the dough. Make sure the folded arms are facing up, and roll the dough away from you into a large rectangle about 1½ inches thick. (Roll in long movements rather than short back-and-forth movements because you want to disperse the butter evenly along the width and the length of the rectangle.) Fold the dough using a double-fold (book-fold) method: Fold the two short edges toward the center leaving a small space in between them (make sure all the edges are aligned and then pinch the dough with your fingertips to seal). Dust off any excess flour. Fold one side of the dough over the other, as though you were closing a book. Dust off any excess flour. One turn is complete. The puff pastry requires five turns in total. Each time you refrigerate the dough mark the number of turns you've completed by indenting the dough with your thumb. Wrap the dough in plastic and refrigerate for 30 minutes.

3. Repeat the rolling, folding, and chilling process an additional three times. When you are ready to begin another turn, make sure to lightly dust the work surface as well as the surface of the dough. Always position the dough with the closed fold on the left, and remember to brush off any excess flour.

4. For the fifth and final turn, fold the dough using the single-fold (letter-fold) method: Fold the bottom third of the dough up and over the center third (pinch the edges to seal), and then fold the top third of dough over the center (pinch the dough to seal the edge). Make sure to align the edges. Dust off any excess flour with a pastry brush.

Pasta Sfoglia Brioche per Cornetto

Croissant Dough

Pasta sfolgia brioche is somewhat similar to a puff pastry in that a butter block is incorporated into a base dough. It also goes through a similar lamination process with the rolling, turning, and folding, but this really belongs to the family of yeasted doughs. It's often used in the preparation of *cornetto* (croissants) or *panini dolci*. My family's favorites are *panini di sfoglia con cioccolato* (chocolate croissants) and *cornetti con crema di mandorle* (croissants with almond cream).

uno PASTELLO (BASE DOUGH)

3⅔ cups (452 g) all-purpose flour, divided

1 tablespoon quick-rising yeast

¼ cup (57 g) superfine sugar

1 teaspoon table salt

seeds of 1 vanilla bean

¾ cup plus 1½ tablespoons (200 ml) cold whole milk

2 large eggs

2 tablespoons unsalted butter, cut into ½-inch pieces

finely grated zest of 1 orange or lemon

due PANETTO (BUTTER BLOCK)

1½ cups (340 g) cold unsalted butter

2 tablespoons all-purpose flour

uno TO MAKE THE BASE DOUGH

1. Reserve ¼ cup (31 g) of the flour. In a stand mixer fitted with the dough hook attachment, mix the remaining flour, yeast, sugar, salt, and vanilla seeds at low speed until well combined.

2. Gradually add the milk, mixing to combine.

3. Add the eggs one at a time, making sure the first egg is incorporated before adding the next.

4. Knead the dough at low speed until the dough forms a ball, about 5 minutes.

5. Add the butter one piece at a time and then add the orange or lemon zest. Continue kneading the dough at low speed until the butter is completely incorporated, and the dough is smooth and begins to form a ball that comes away from the sides of the bowl, 5 to 6 minutes. (The dough should be sticky, but if more dough is sticking to the sides of the bowl than to the ball, add the reserved ¼ cup flour 1 tablespoon at a time until it comes together.) Transfer the dough to a sheet of plastic wrap, shape into a rectangle, then wrap with the plastic. Refrigerate for 1 hour.

due TO PREPARE THE BUTTER BLOCK

1. Place the butter sticks side by side, touching each other, on a lightly floured work surface. Lightly flour the surface of the butter. Using a lightly floured rolling pin, bang and roll the butter to flatten, incorporating the flour and joining the sticks together. Shape the butter into a 7-inch square. If needed, lightly flour the butter occasionally when rolling and shaping.

2. Wrap the butter block in plastic and refrigerate for at least 30 minutes.

tre TO PREPARE THE _PACHETTO_ (DOUGH PACKAGE)

1. Remove the dough from the refrigerator, unwrap, and transfer the dough to a clean, lightly floured work surface. Lightly dust the rolling pin with flour and roll the cold dough into an 11-inch square. Unwrap the butter square and place it diagonally on top of the dough square. Fold one outside corner of dough in toward the center and bring the opposite corner of dough in and over so that they meet in the middle and overlap. Pinch the edges of the dough to seal. Repeat with the other two corners. The butter should be completely enclosed and edges completely sealed.

2. If needed, dust the work surface and the surface of the dough package with flour. Using a lightly floured rolling pin and, holding it with a hand at each end, gently tap the surface of the dough, seam side up, to flatten until the square becomes larger and the butter begins to become more pliable. Then, roll the dough (using long movements rather than short back-and-forth movements) to ⅓ inch thickness. (Lift the dough up occasionally and dust the work surface lightly with flour to prevent the dough from sticking.)

3. Fold the dough using the single-fold (letter-fold) method: Fold the bottom third of dough up and over the center third (pinch the edges to seal) and then fold the top third of the dough over the center (pinch the edges to seal). Brush off any excess flour with a pastry brush. One turn is complete. (If the butter has softened, refrigerate the dough for 30 minutes before proceeding.)

4. Make another turn. Starting from the narrow end, roll the dough to ⅓ inch thickness. Fold using the single-fold (letter-fold) method without sealing the edges. Dust off any excess flour with a pastry brush. Two turns are complete. Wrap the dough in plastic and refrigerate for 2 hours.

5. Remove the dough from the refrigerator and lightly dust the work surface and also the surface of the dough with flour. Repeat Step 4, completing 1 turn and fold using the single-fold method without sealing edges. Dust off any excess flour with a pastry brush. Wrap the dough in plastic and refrigerate for 1 hour. Three turns are complete.

6. Remove the dough from the refrigerator and lightly dust the work surface and the surface of the dough with flour. Repeat Step 4, completing 1 turn and fold using the single-fold method without sealing the edges. Dust off any excess flour with a pastry brush. Wrap the dough in plastic and refrigerate for 1 hour. The fourth and final turn is complete. Refrigerate until cold.

7. If not using immediately, the dough can be stored, well wrapped in parchment paper, then in plastic, and then in an airtight container in the refrigerator, for up to 2 days or in the freezer for 3 to 4 weeks.

Pasta Choux

Choux Pastry

Pasta choux (choux pastry) is a precooked paste that is shaped and baked in the oven. *Pasta choux* paste is simply made by cooking water, flour, and eggs and vigorously stirring until smooth. The soft paste is piped from a pastry bag to create different shapes. During baking, steam releases from the dough, causing it to expand into a light and crispy hollow shell often referred to as a "bun." The more popular shapes are the *bignè* (cream puffs or profiteroles) or éclairs. The buns are often filled with various creams like Crema Chantilly (page 12), Crema Pasticcera (page 10), or gelato. The filled buns can be simply topped with confectioner's sugar or more decadently with *crema ganache* (chocolate ganache), caramel, or fruit coulis.

Choux buns can be made in advance but should be filled just prior to serving. Store choux buns in resealable bags at room temperature for up to two days or in an airtight container in the freezer for up to one month. When ready to use, defrost and warm in a preheated 350°F (180°C) oven for a few minutes until crisp.

> 1 cup (240 ml) water
>
> ½ cup (113 g) unsalted butter, cut into 16 equal pieces
>
> 2 teaspoons sugar
>
> ½ teaspoon salt
>
> 1 cup plus 2 tablespoons (140 g) all-purpose flour, sifted
>
> 4 large eggs, at room temperature

1. In a medium saucepan, bring the water, butter, sugar, and salt to a rolling boil over medium-high heat, stirring gently with a wooden spoon.

2. When the mixture begins to boil, add the flour all at once and stir vigorously until the paste reaches an internal temperature of 175°F (80°C), pulls away from the sides of the pan, and forms a ball, about 1 minute. Remove from the heat.

3. Allow the paste to cool, stirring a couple of times, to a temperature of 120°F (50°C), about 2 minutes.

4. Add the eggs one at a time, making sure each egg is well incorporated before adding the next, stirring vigorously until well combined and the paste is smooth.

Cakes and Cheesecakes

Torta all'Arancia

Orange Cake

This light, moist, citrusy cake is one of my favorites. It rises nice and high and it's very easy to make. I especially enjoy serving it at coffee time. When I was working, I would get a call from my sister almost every day in the late afternoon and she would ask, "Coffee time?" My answer was always yes! We would go to our mother's house, where we were always greeted with the most amazing aroma of freshly percolated coffee, *pizzelle*, or cakes just like this one. And we never left empty-handed. My mother would send us on our way with freshly made *sugo di pomodoro* (tomato sauce), lasagne, cannelloni, or fresh bread. I look forward to these types of rituals, not because of all the goodies, but because it's a time to catch up and spend quality time with my family. I believe it's one of the reasons our large family remains so close.

uno CAKE

6 large eggs

2 cups (250 g) all-purpose flour

4 teaspoons baking powder

½ teaspoon salt

½ cup (120 ml) vegetable oil

1 teaspoon pure vanilla extract

1 cup plus 2 tablespoons (255 g) superfine sugar, divided

grated zest of 2 oranges

1 cup (240 ml) freshly squeezed orange juice

¼ teaspoon cream of tartar

due SYRUP

1½ cups (355 ml) freshly squeezed orange juice

½ cup (113 g) superfine sugar

zest of 1 orange in large strips (make sure no pith is attached)

½ vanilla bean, split and seeded

2 to 3 tablespoons Cointreau or other orange liqueur

uno TO MAKE THE CAKE

1. Separate the cold eggs. Place the yolks in a large bowl and the whites in a stand mixer. Cover each bowl with plastic wrap and allow the eggs to come to room temperature, about 30 minutes.

2. Preheat the oven to 350°F (180°C). Very lightly coat with butter the bottom and sides of a 10-inch tube pan with feet and removable bottom.

3. Using a fine-mesh sieve, sift together the flour, baking powder, and salt into a medium bowl. Whisk to combine well.

4. Use a handheld mixer to beat the egg yolks, oil, vanilla, and 1 cup (225 g) sugar on medium speed until light and fluffy, about 2 minutes.

5. Beat in the orange zest and juice.

6. Reduce the mixer speed to low and gradually add the flour mixture, beating to just combine (do not overmix).

7. In a stand mixer fitted with the whip attachment, beat the egg whites to stiff peaks, beginning at low speed and gradually increasing to medium-high. When the whites are foamy, add the cream of tartar. At the soft-peak stage, add the remaining 2 tablespoons (30 g) sugar.

8. Using a large flexible spatula, fold one-third of the egg whites into the egg yolk mixture to lighten the batter, then carefully fold in the remaining egg whites until just combined.

9. Pour the batter into the prepared pan, spreading it evenly with an offset spatula.

10. Bake until golden and a cake tester inserted into the center comes out clean, 50 to 60 minutes.

11. Remove from the oven and immediately invert the pan onto a wire rack. Let the cake cool completely in the pan upside down on the rack.

12. While the cake bakes, prepare the orange syrup.

due TO MAKE THE SYRUP

1. In a small saucepan over medium heat, bring the orange juice, sugar, orange zest, and the vanilla bean and seeds to a simmer, stirring until the sugar dissolves, about 5 minutes.

2. Reduce the heat to low, add the liqueur, and continue to simmer until the syrup reduces and thickens slightly about 5 minutes.

3. Remove from the heat and strain the syrup through a fine-mesh sieve into a pourable container. Allow the syrup to cool slightly.

tre TO ASSEMBLE AND SERVE

1. Flip the cake pan over, carefully run a thin knife around the edges of the pan, and turn the cake out onto a serving plate or cake stand.

2. To serve, place the cake on dessert plates and serve with warm orange syrup.

Torta Millefoglie con Crema Pasticcera al Cioccolato Fondente e Cioccolato Bianco

Puff Pastry Cake with Dark and White Chocolate Pastry Cream

To make this *torta*, you'll need 2 (8 x 1-inch) round mousse rings. If you do not have mousse rings, you can use the sides of two 8-inch springform pans.

uno PASTA SFOGLIA (PUFF PASTRY) DISKS

confectioners' sugar, for dusting

⅔ pound (300 g) freshly made Pasta Sfolgia (page 22), or 3 precut sheets (1½ pounds, 675 g) thawed store-bought puff pastry

due CREMA PASTICCERA AL CIOCCOLATO FONDENTE (DARK CHOCOLATE PASTRY CREAM)

2 sheets (3.3 g) gold gelatin leaves

1½ cups (125 g) Crema Pasticcera 2 (page 12)

4 ounces (113 g) good-quality bittersweet chocolate, finely chopped

1 cup plus 2 tablespoons (270 ml) heavy cream

⅓ cup (41 g) confectioners' sugar, sifted

tre CREMA PASTICCERA AL CIOCCOLATO BIANCO (WHITE CHOCOLATE PASTRY CREAM)

2 sheets (3.3 g) gold gelatin sheets

1½ cups (125 g) prepared Crema Pasticcera 2 (page 12)

3 ounces (75 g) good-quality white chocolate

1 cup plus 2 tablespoons (270 ml) heavy cream

finale ASSEMBLY

fresh fruit

Chocolate Curls (page 171)

confectioners' sugar, for dusting (optional)

uno TO MAKE THE PUFF PASTRY DISKS

1. Position a rack in the middle of the oven. Preheat the oven to 500°F (260°C). Line three rimmed baking sheets with parchment paper. Using a fine-mesh sieve, sift confectioners' sugar over the parchment paper to lightly coat.

2. If using homemade pasta sfoglia, cut it into 3 (3½ ounce) portions.

3. Working with one sheet at a time, roll one portion of dough (homemade) or sheet of pastry (store-bought) to ⅛ inch thick. Using a 9-inch ring mold, baking pan, or springform pan as a guide, cut out a pastry disk. (The pastry tends to shrink, even after chilling, so I find it better to cut out a larger disk than I'll actually need; if necessary, once the pastry is baked and cooled, trim to 8 inches.) Using a rolling pin, carefully transfer the disk of pastry to a prepared baking sheet. To prevent the dough from rising, poke holes all over the pastry with a fork and then transfer to the freezer to chill for 30 minutes. Repeat with the other 2 dough portions or sheets.

4. Work with one disk of pastry at a time, and keep the remaining disks in the freezer. Use a fine-mesh sieve to generously coat the surface of the pastry disk with confectioners' sugar. Cover the disk with a sheet of parchment paper and lay a second baking sheet on top, and weigh it down with a ceramic dish.

5. Bake until the pastry is crispy and golden, 25 to 30 minutes.

6. Remove from the oven, transfer the baking sheet to a wire rack, and allow the pastry to cool on the baking sheet for a few minutes. Then transfer the pastry disk to a wire rack to cool completely.

7. Repeat with the remaining pastry disks.

due TO MAKE THE DARK CHOCOLATE PASTRY CREAM

1. Line a rimmed baking sheet with parchment paper or a silicone baking mat and place 1 (8 x 1-inch) round mousse ring on top. Place a sheet of plastic wrap into the mold, making sure there is a 2-inch overhang. Smooth out the plastic.

2. Soak the gelatin in a small bowl of cold water until softened, about 15 minutes.

3. Warm the pastry cream over low heat to a temperature of 95°F (35°C).

4. Add the chocolate, stirring constantly, until the custard is smooth and reaches a temperature of 105°F (40°C). Remove from the heat.

5. Immediately remove the gelatin sheets from the water, squeeze out the excess liquid, and add to the chocolate custard, stirring until dissolved.

6. Transfer the custard to a small bowl, stirring occasionally to prevent a skin from forming as it cools to a temperature of 86°F (30°C). Strain the custard through a fine-mesh sieve into a medium bowl.

7. Meanwhile in another medium bowl, use a handheld mixer to beat together the heavy cream and confectioners' sugar at high speed to stiff peaks.

8. Fold one-third of the whipped cream into the cooled custard to loosen the mixture, then fold in the remaining whipped cream in two additions.

9. Transfer the mixture to the prepared mold. Use a small offset spatula to spread and smooth out the surface.

10. Chill the custard in the freezer until firm, 4 to 6 hours, or preferably overnight.

tre TO MAKE THE WHITE CHOCOLATE PASTRY CREAM

1. Follow the directions for the dark chocolate pastry cream, using white chocolate instead of bittersweet and omitting the sugar.

finale TO ASSEMBLE AND SERVE

1. Stack the 3 pastry disks on top of each other and trim them with a sharp knife so they are all the same size. Brush off any crumbs with a pastry brush. Set aside the best-looking disk to top the cake.

2. Remove the frozen disk of dark chocolate pastry cream from the freezer. Remove the ring mold. For best presentation and to prevent the chocolate disk from breaking, place one disk of pastry bottom-side up on top of the chocolate custard disk, then flip the pastry and chocolate disks together so that the chocolate disk is facing up. Remove the plastic wrap and transfer to a cake plate or stand. (Handling the disks in this manner makes it much easier to center the chocolate disks on the pastry disks. The less the chocolate disks are handled the better because it eliminates the chances of smudges and breakage.)

3. Repeat with the second disk of pastry and the disk of white chocolate custard. Stack on the dark chocolate disk.

4. Top with the remaining pastry disk. Transfer to the refrigerator to thaw the pastry cream.

5. To serve, remove from refrigerator and garnish with fresh fruit and chocolate curls. Lightly dust with confectioners' sugar, if using. Serve with extra fruit on the side.

Puff Pastry Cake with Dark and White Chocolate Pastry Cream

Torta Caprese

MAKES 1 (10-INCH) ROUND CAKE

Flourless Chocolate Torte with Almonds and Hazelnuts

Torta caprese is a traditional flourless chocolate and almond cake from Napoli (Naples). It's often called *uno dei pasticci piu fortunati della storia*, or "one of history's most fortunate mistakes." Apparently, the original baker forgot to add flour to the batter. It's named after the island of Capri where the cake first originated. The cake is moist and full of flavor with a crisp outer crust. It's traditionally served with a light dusting of confectioners' sugar, but mine has almonds, hazelnuts, and a dusting of sweetened cocoa.

I keep a cardboard round handy for cakes like this one that need to be inverted while still warm. I place a sheet of parchment paper on top of the cake, then the cardboard round; then I flip the cake over, and remove the pan and parchment paper. Then I place parchment paper over the base of the cake, then a wire rack, and then I flip again. I find this method works quite well, and thankfully I haven't had a cake fall apart yet.

> 6 large eggs
>
> 7 ounces (200 g) good-quality dark chocolate, 70%, or bittersweet, 60%
>
> ¾ cup plus 2 tablespoons (200 g) unsalted butter
>
> 1 tablespoon unsweetened cocoa powder, sifted
>
> ¾ cup plus 2 tablespoons (200 g) superfine sugar
>
> ¼ teaspoon salt
>
> 1⅓ cups (200 g) toasted almonds, finely ground
>
> ⅔ cup (100 g) toasted hazelnuts, finely ground
>
> 1 (16-gram) package lievito vaniglinato (yeast for cake with vanilla) (see page 8)
>
> cocoa powder or confectioners' sugar, for dusting (optional)
>
> Sweetened Whipped Cream (page 13), to serve (optional)

1. Separate the eggs. Place the yolks in a small bowl or liquid measuring cup and the whites in a medium bowl. Cover both bowls with plastic wrap and allow the eggs to come to room temperature, about 30 minutes.

2. Preheat the oven to 350°F (180°C). Using a pastry brush, coat a 10-inch round cake pan with butter. Line the base of the pan with a parchment paper round, and lightly butter the paper. Dust the base and sides of the cake pan with unsweetened cocoa powder and tap out any excess cocoa.

3. In a heatproof bowl set over a saucepan of just-simmering water (do not let the bowl touch the water), stir together the chocolate and butter until both have melted and the mixture is smooth.

4. Remove from the heat, add the cocoa powder, and stir to combine. Set aside to cool for 3 minutes.

5. Add the egg yolks and stir with a wooden spoon to combine well. Gradually add the sugar and salt, stirring to combine well. Add the nuts and stir to just combine. Add the yeast, stirring to combine well.

6. Using a handheld mixer, beat the egg whites at high speed to soft peaks.

34 GRACE'S SWEET LIFE

7. Using a large flexible spatula, fold the egg whites into the chocolate mixture in three additions just to combine.

8. Transfer the cake batter to the prepared pan. Tap the filled pan on the counter a couple of times to release any air bubbles that may have formed.

9. Bake until a cake tester inserted into the center comes out with just a few moist crumbs attached, 45 to 55 minutes (begin testing the cake at 45 minutes), rotating the pan halfway through baking. Do not open the oven door within the first 15 minutes of baking.

10. Transfer the cake to a wire rack and allow the cake to cool in the pan for 5 minutes. Carefully remove from the pan, remove the parchment paper, and return to the wire rack to cool completely.

11. Transfer the cake to a cake plate or cake stand. Dust with cocoa, or the more traditional confectioners' sugar, and serve with whipped cream.

Flourless Chocolate Torte
with Almonds and Hazelnuts

Torta Paradiso

Paradise Cake

Torta paradiso is one of the more traditional Italian cakes originating from the Lombardy region, and there are several stories surrounding its origin. According to one legend, a monk from Certosa di Pavia (a monastery in the small town of Pavia) used to sneak out of the monastery and wander the countryside searching for herbs with healing powers. On one of his secret escapades, he met a young bride and apparently she taught him the recipe. Unfortunately, it was discovered that he had been sneaking out, which was against the monastery's very strict rules. He was imprisoned within the walls of the monastery, where he had to dedicate his time to preparing the cake. His only consolation was that every time he made the cake he was reminded of the beautiful young woman who taught him how to prepare it. All the brothers in the monastery loved the tender cake, and they named it *paradiso*.

It's a very simple cake to prepare and is quite similar to a sponge cake, but butter is incorporated into the batter. It's classically dusted heavily with confectioners' sugar and often prepared for birthdays.

> 6 large egg yolks
>
> 4 large egg whites
>
> ¾ cup plus 3 tablespoons (150 g) potato starch or cornstarch
>
> 1 cup plus 3 tablespoons (150 g) all-purpose flour
>
> ½ package (8 g) lievito vaniglinato (yeast for cake) (see page 8)
>
> 1⅓ cups (300 g) butter, at room temperature (very soft), plus more for the pan
>
> 2¼ cups plus 2½ tablespoons (300 g) confectioners' sugar, divided
>
> seeds from 1 vanilla bean, or 2 teaspoons pure vanilla extract
>
> zest of 1 lemon
>
> pinch of salt
>
> confectioners' sugar, sifted, for dusting
>
> fresh fruit or berry compote and Sweetened Whipped Cream (page 13), to serve

1. Place the egg yolks in a small bowl and the egg whites in a large bowl; cover each bowl with plastic wrap, and allow the eggs to come to room temperature, about 30 minutes.

2. Preheat the oven to 350°F (180°C). Butter the base and sides of a 10 x 3-inch round cake pan. Line the base and sides of the pan with parchment paper. (The crust on the sides of the cake is very delicate; for the best presentation, lining the sides will prevent the cake from sticking.) Lightly butter the paper.

3. Using a fine-mesh sieve, sift the potato starch or cornstarch, flour, and yeast into a medium bowl. Whisk to combine well, and set aside.

4. In a stand mixer fitted with the paddle attachment, beat the butter, one-half of the confectioners' sugar, the vanilla seeds or vanilla extract, and the lemon zest at medium speed until creamy, pale, and smooth, about 6 minutes. Add the egg yolks one at a time and continue beating at medium

speed, making sure each egg is well incorporated before adding the next (take your time adding the yolks) until creamy, about 3 minutes.

5. Beat the egg whites and salt with a handheld mixer at high speed. When the egg whites reach a soft peak, reduce the mixer speed to medium low and gradually add the remaining confectioners' sugar. Increase the mixer speed to high and continue to beat to stiff peaks.

6. Carefully fold the egg whites into the cake batter with a large flexible spatula in three additions.

7. Transfer the batter to the prepared cake pan and use an offset spatula to spread the batter to the sides of the pan. Tap the cake pan on the counter to release any air bubbles.

8. Bake until golden and a cake tester inserted into the center comes out clean, 45 to 55 minutes, rotating the baking pan halfway through the baking time.

9. Transfer the cake to a wire rack and cool in the pan for about 25 minutes.

10. Carefully remove the parchment from the sides of the pan. To remove the cake from the cake tin, place a sheet of parchment on top of the cake pan (to cover). Place a 10-inch round cake board on top of the parchment paper, flip the cake pan over and remove the parchment on the bottom of the cake. Place a sheet of parchment on the bottom of the cake that is now facing up, lay the wire rack on top of the parchment and flip the cake back over so that the base of the cake is now resting on the wire rack. Let stand on the wire rack until cooled completely.

11. Using a fine-mesh sieve, sift a generous amount of confectioners' sugar on top of the cake. Transfer to a cake plate. Serve with fresh fruit or berry compote and whipped cream.

Paradise Cake

Chiffon Cake with Orange Chantilly Cream and Orange Cream

Torta Chiffon all'Arancia con Crema Chantilly all'Arancia e Crema all'Arancia

Chiffon Cake with Orange Chantilly Cream and Orange Cream

This orange-flavored cake is filled with orange chantilly cream, iced with orange cream and orange chantilly cream, and garnished with a candied orange slice. It can also be enjoyed in a simpler version by baking the cake in a dry (unbuttered) tube pan. Instead of layering, filling, and decorating with both creams, you can simply dust with confectioners' sugar to serve. For the best flavor, begin preparing the orange chantilly cream the day before assembling the cake to allow the vanilla to infuse in the cream. Unlike other chantilly creams, this one is stabilized with gelatin so it holds its shape for piping and doesn't melt and weep as easily. The syrup from the candied orange slices is great in iced tea. For a special treat, dip half of each candied orange slice in melted chocolate and set aside to set. Note that this recipe gives the option of using orange-flavored bakery emulsion. Bakery emulsions are a water-based and alcohol-free alternative to extracts. They are gluten free and can be used interchangeably with extracts.

uno TORTA CHIFFON ALL'ARANCIA (ORANGE CHIFFON CAKE)

7 large eggs

vegetable oil spray, for coating the pan

1½ cups (340 g) superfine sugar, divided

2¾ cups (340 g) all-purpose flour

3 teaspoons baking powder

pinch of salt

½ cup (120 ml) vegetable oil or canola oil

¾ cup (180 ml) freshly squeezed orange juice (from 2 to 3 oranges)

grated zest of 1 orange

2 teaspoons pure vanilla extract

due CREMA CHANTILLY ALL'ARANCIA (ORANGE CHANTILLY CREAM)

3 cups (720 ml) heavy cream

1½ vanilla beans, split and seeded

¼ cup (60 ml) very cold water

2 teaspoons unflavored powdered gelatin

grated zest of 1 orange or ¼ to ½ teaspoon orange extract or bakery emulsion

1 cup (125 g) confectioners' sugar, sifted

tre CREMA ALL'ARANCIA (ORANGE CREAM)

zest of 1 orange, cut in strips with pith removed

1½ cups (355 ml) freshly squeezed orange juice (from about 6 oranges)

½ cup (120 ml) heavy cream

1 vanilla bean, split and seeded

6 large egg yolks, at room temperature

¾ cup plus 3½ teaspoons (185 g) superfine sugar

¼ cup plus 2½ tablespoons (51 g) all-purpose flour

quattro FETTINE DI ARANCIA CANDITA CON VANIGLIA
(CANDIED ORANGE SLICES WITH VANILLA)

1 large orange

1½ cups (360 ml) water

1½ cups (338 g) superfine sugar

½ vanilla bean, split and seeded

finale ASSEMBLY

1 tablespoon liqueur, like Kirsch or Grand Marnier (optional)

uno TO MAKE THE ORANGE CHIFFON CAKE

1. Separate the eggs, placing the egg yolks in a large bowl and the whites in a small bowl. Cover each bowl with plastic wrap and allow the eggs to come to room temperature, about 30 minutes. (It's important to bring the egg whites to room temperature because if they are too cold there's a danger of overmixing the whites, creating big air bubbles which will then break when you fold the whites into the cake batter.)

2. Preheat the oven to 350°F (180°C). Very lightly coat a 10-inch round baking pan with vegetable oil spray and line the base with a circle of parchment paper.

3. Reserve ¼ cup (57 g) of the sugar. Using a fine-mesh sieve, sift the flour, baking powder, and salt into the bowl of a stand mixer; add the sugar and fit the mixer with the paddle attachment. Stir on low speed until well combined.

4. Gradually add the oil to the egg yolks, whisking constantly.

5. Gradually whisk in the orange juice, then whisk in the orange zest and vanilla.

6. Add the egg yolk mixture to the dry ingredients all at once. Mix on low speed to aerate the batter until most of the dry ingredients are moistened, about 20 seconds. Increase the speed to medium and blend until the batter is smooth, about 30 seconds.

7. Remove the bowl from the mixer and use a large flexible spatula to scrape the sides and bottom of the bowl and the paddle attachment. Return the bowl to the mixer and mix on medium speed until smooth, 30 to 45 seconds.

8. Transfer the batter to a large bowl. Wash and dry the mixer bowl, making sure the bowl is dried thoroughly and no trace of batter remains.

9. In the stand mixer fitted with the whip attachment, beat the egg whites on low speed for 30 seconds, then increase the speed to medium and beat until foamy.

10. With the mixer running at medium speed, gradually add the reserved ¼ cup (57 g) sugar down the side of the bowl 1 tablespoon at a time and beat to soft peaks, about 2 minutes.

11. Using a large flexible spatula, stir one-third of the egg white mixture into the batter. Very carefully fold the remaining egg whites into the batter in two additions until all the egg white streaks are gone and the batter is a uniform color.

12. Transfer the cake batter to the prepared baking pan and level with an offset spatula.

13. Bake until golden and a cake tester inserted into the center comes out clean, 45 to 60 minutes. (Begin testing the cake for doneness at the 45-minute mark but no sooner. Do not open the oven door within the first 45 minutes of baking.)

14. Transfer the cake to a wire rack and cool in the pan for 45 minutes. Remove the cake from the pan and transfer directly to the wire rack to cool completely.

15. When the cake is completely cool, wrap it in plastic wrap and refrigerate for at least 4 hours, or up to 1 day. Before cutting the cake layers to assemble the cake, wrap in plastic and freeze for no longer than 30 minutes. (It is much easier to trim and cut the cake into layers when it is well chilled, but it is important for the cake to be completely cooled before freezing.)

due TO MAKE THE ORANGE CHANTILLY CREAM

1. Stir together the cream and the vanilla bean and seeds in an airtight container, cover, and refrigerate to allow the vanilla to infuse for 24 hours. (Less time is fine, but the longer the vanilla is allowed to infuse, the better the flavor will be.)

2. About 15 minutes before preparing the chantilly cream, place the bowl of a stand mixer and the whip attachment, or another large metal bowl and a large balloon whisk or the beaters of a handheld mixer, in the freezer.

3. Place the very cold water in a small saucepan, and sprinkle the gelatin in while whisking with a fork. Set aside to bloom, about 5 minutes. Place the saucepan over low heat and stir until the gelatin is dissolved. Remove from the heat and set aside to cool.

4. Remove the bowl and whip or beaters from the freezer. Attach the bowl to a mixer and fit with the whip attachment.

5. Remove the vanilla-infused cream from the refrigerator and strain through a fine-mesh sieve into the cold bowl (discard the vanilla bean). Strain the cooled gelatin through a fine-mesh sieve into a small pourable container.

6. Beat the cream on low speed for 30 seconds, then increase the speed to medium and beat for 30 seconds. Increase the speed to high, add the orange zest or extract (or bakery emulsion), and then gradually add the sugar down the side of the bowl and beat to very soft peaks, about 2 minutes. With

the mixer running on high speed, gradually add the gelatin and continue to beat to stiff peaks, about 2 minutes.

7. Transfer to an airtight container and then refrigerate until ready to use.

tre TO MAKE THE ORANGE CREAM

1. In a small saucepan over medium heat, bring the orange zest and juice, cream, and vanilla bean and seeds just to a boil. Remove from the heat, cover, and allow the vanilla and orange zest to infuse for 10 to 12 minutes.

2. In a medium bowl, whisk the egg yolks and sugar until pale in color. Add the flour and whisk to combine well.

3. Gradually add the hot orange cream mixture to the lightened egg yolks in a slow, steady stream, whisking constantly until well combined. Transfer the mixture to the saucepan.

4. Cook over medium heat, stirring constantly, until thickened, 3 to 5 minutes.

5. Remove from the heat and strain through a fine-mesh sieve into a 9 x 13-inch baking dish. Use an offset spatula to spread the cream to the edges of the pan. Place a sheet of plastic wrap directly onto the surface and set aside to cool completely.

quattro TO MAKE THE CANDIED ORANGE SLICES WITH VANILLA

1. To prepare an ice water bath, fill a large bowl half full with ice and cover the ice with cold water. Line a rimmed baking sheet with parchment paper.

2. Wash and cut the orange (do not peel) into thin slices with a sharp knife or a mandoline. Remove and discard the seeds and the end slices.

3. In a medium skillet over medium heat, bring the water, sugar, and the vanilla bean and seeds to a boil, stirring until the sugar is dissolved and the mixture is clear.

4. Reduce the heat to medium-low and add the orange slices in a single layer. Simmer, uncovered, turning the slices occasionally, until translucent, about 1 hour.

5. Using a slotted spoon, transfer the orange slices to the prepared baking sheet and allow to cool completely. Discard the vanilla bean and set the syrup aside to cool.

finale TO ASSEMBLE AND SERVE

1. Preheat the oven to 375°F (190°C). Line a rimmed baking sheet with parchment paper. Remove the cake from the freezer. If the top of the cake is uneven, use a large serrated knife to trim the top level. Reserve the trimmings.

2. Cut the cake into 3 even layers. Set the middle layer aside.

3. Stir the liqueur into the reserved cooled orange syrup from the candied orange slices. Using a pastry brush, brush the cut side of the top and bottom cake layers with syrup. Return the 2 layers (unwrapped) to the freezer or refrigerator (to set the syrup).

4. Cut the middle cake layer and any reserved trimmings into small pieces. Transfer to the baking sheet and bake until toasted and dry, 8 to 12 minutes. (Keep a watchful eye as they toast, because you don't want the pieces to color.) Remove from the oven and transfer to a wire rack to cool completely. Transfer the dry cake pieces to a food processor or blender and process to fine crumbs.

5. Transfer the orange cream to a large pastry bag fitted with a round plain tip (like a Wilton 1A). If you find the cream is extremely soft, refrigerate the filled piping bag for about 15 minutes to firm up the cream and allow it to hold its shaped when piped; be sure to keep a watchful eye because if it chills too long, the cream will be difficult to pipe.

6. Remove the orange chantilly cream from the refrigerator, transfer half to a large pastry bag fitted with a decorative tip (like a Wilton 1M) and transfer 1 cup to a small bowl (for crumb coat).

7. Remove the cake layers from the freezer. Place the bottom cake layer cut-side up on a 10-inch round cake board.

8. Pipe the orange chantilly cream around the edge of the bottom cake layer to create a border. Pipe the orange chantilly cream inside of the border, completely covering the bottom cake layer. Use an offset spatula to evenly smooth the cream to the border.

9. Place the leveled top layer cut-side down (if you had to trim the top of the cake initially to level, keep the trimmed side up) over the orange chantilly cream, pressing down gently to adhere.

10. Chill the remaining orange chantilly cream in between uses. To crumb coat the cake, use an offset spatula to spread a thin layer of the reserved 1 cup orange chantilly cream over the top cake layer, spreading to the edges, and then spread a thin layer on the sides of the cake, pressing firmly and evenly with the spatula. Use your spatula to round off the edges and to remove any excess icing. Refrigerate to set, about 20 minutes.

11. Remove the cake from the refrigerator. Place a baking sheet on your work surface. Transfer the cooled cake crumbs to a medium bowl.

12. Using an offset spatula, spread a thin layer of orange chantilly cream on the top and sides of the cake. Immediately, while the orange chantilly cream is still soft, lift and hold the cake with one hand over the baking sheet, making sure your hand is in the center of the cake board for stability. Slightly tilt the cake, and with your free hand scoop crumbs and press them into the sides of the cake, making sure the sides are completely covered and the crumbs are evenly distributed. Allow excess crumbs to drop onto the baking sheet.

13. To decorate the top of the cake, working from left to right and starting ⅛ inch in from the edge of the cake, alternate piping vertical stripes of orange chantilly cream and orange cream, leaving about ⅛ inch between each stripe. Place a cooled candied orange slice in the center of the cake.

14. To serve, transfer the cake to a cake stand or plate. Store in an airtight container in the refrigerator.

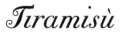

Tiramisù

Tiramisu

This tiramisu recipe is almost authentic, but I decorate mine with mounds of whipped cream, whereas in the classical presentation, a portion of the mascarpone cream is reserved and piped in rosettes. Because tiramisu is prepared with raw eggs, please use the freshest eggs possible. Good-quality *savoiardi* are available at Italian delis and grocers; supermarket ladyfingers are not substantial enough to soak in the liquid for tiramisu.

uno CREMA DI MASCARPONE (MASCARPONE CREAM)

6 large eggs, divided, at room temperature

pinch of salt

⅔ cup (150 g) superfine sugar, divided

1 teaspoon pure vanilla extract

2½ cups (500 g) mascarpone cheese, at room temperature

1 to 2 tablespoons (15 to 30 ml) strong espresso, cooled (optional)

finale ASSEMBLY

1½ cups (355 ml) strong espresso, cooled (sweetened, if desired, sugar should be added when hot to dissolve)

marsala wine or rum, (optional)

8½ ounces (240 g) savoiardi biscuits (ladyfingers), about 24 cookies

unsweetened cocoa, for dusting

Sweetened Whipped Cream (page 13) (optional)

bittersweet chocolate bar, chilled in the freezer, for garnish (optional)

uno TO MAKE THE MASCARPONE CREAM

1. In a stand mixer fitted with the whip attachment, whisk the egg whites to very stiff peaks, beginning at low speed and gradually increasing to high, about 13 minutes total. When the egg whites are foamy, add the salt. When the egg whites reach soft peaks, reduce the speed to low, and gradually add ⅓ cup (75 g) of the sugar, 1 tablespoon at a time, then return the mixer to high speed after each addition to combine well. After all of the sugar has been added, return to high speed to continue beating to very stiff peaks.

2. In a large bowl, whisk the egg yolks, vanilla, and the remaining ⅓ cup (75 g) sugar until thick and pale in color.

3. In a small bowl, stir the mascarpone with a wooden spoon until smooth. Do not overmix.

4. Add the mascarpone to the egg yolk mixture in three additions, whisking just to combine. Do not overmix. If using, add the espresso ½ tablespoon at a time, taste, and add more if desired. Don't add more than 2 tablespoons or the consistency of the cream will become too thin.

5. Fold the whipped egg whites into the mascarpone mixture in three additions, incorporating each addition well before adding the next.

finale TO ASSEMBLE AND SERVE

1. Place the espresso into a small shallow bowl. Add the wine or rum to taste, if using, and stir to combine. Dip the *savoiardi* biscuits one at a time into the espresso for a couple of seconds. (Do not soak the biscuits for too long or they will become mushy and fall apart.) Place the biscuit lengthwise in an 8 x 12-inch baking dish. If necessary, cut the biscuits (before soaking) to fit. Repeat until the bottom of the dish is covered.

2. Spread half of the mascarpone cream evenly over the layer of *savoiardi* biscuits.

3. Using a small fine-mesh sieve, evenly dust a generous amount of cocoa over top of the mascarpone cream.

4. Arrange another layer of espresso-dipped savoiardi biscuits perpendicular to the first layer over the top of the mascarpone cream. Again, if necessary, cut the cookies to fit.

5. Spread the remaining mascarpone cream evenly over the layer of biscuits. Again, using a small, fine-mesh sieve, evenly dust a generous amount of cocoa.

6. Cover the tiramisu with plastic wrap and refrigerate for at least 3 hours and up to 8 hours.

7. To serve the tiramisu, transfer the whipped cream to a large pastry bag fitted with a plain tip. Remove the tiramisu from the refrigerator and pipe mounds on top of the mascarpone cream. To garnish, using a fine rasp grater, grate the chocolate over the tiramisu.

Tiramisu

Fiadone Dolce di Ricotta

MAKES 2 (9-INCH) CAKES

Abruzzo Sweet Cheesecake

Fiadone is a sweet ricotta cake from the Abruzzo region and is typically prepared and served at Easter. *Fiadone* means "to swell," and the name is fitting because the cake expands as it bakes, so it is very important to not cover the filling completely with pastry. The cakes must be baked immediately after the ricotta filling is prepared. Prepare the pastry strips just before making the filling.

uno SWEET PASTRY CRUST

    2 (13-inch) disks Pasta Frolla 2 (Sweet Pastry Dough) (page 19)

due SWEET RICOTTA FILLING

    12 large eggs, separated, at room temperature

    1 cup plus 1 tablespoon (240 g) superfine sugar

    4 cups (1 kilogram) ricotta cheese, drained overnight

    grated zest of 1 lemon, or 1 ounce (30 ml) rum

finale ASSEMBLY

    1 large egg, lightly beaten, for egg wash (if using sanding sugar)

    clear sanding sugar (coarse sugar) (optional)

    confectioners' sugar, to serve (optional)

uno TO MAKE THE SWEET PASTRY CRUST

1. Working with one disk of dough at a time, transfer the disk to a lightly floured work surface and roll out the dough to ⅛ inch thick. Cut a 13-inch circle (to line the pan with; use the remaining dough for decorative strips).

2. Lightly spray 2 (9-inch) springform pans with cooking spray. Line each pan with dough, allowing the excess to hang over the edges and making sure there are no holes in the pastry. Using a scalloped pastry wheel, cut 9 (¼ x ½-inch) strips of dough. Cover the dough-lined pans and pastry strips with a kitchen towel to prevent the pastry from drying out.

due TO MAKE THE SWEET RICOTTA FILLING

1. Preheat the oven to 350°F (180°C). Place the egg yolks in a stand mixer and the whites in a large bowl.

2. In a stand mixer fitted with the whisk attachment, beat the egg yolks and sugar on high speed for 2 minutes.

3. Remove the bowl from the mixer. Use a balloon whisk to whip in the ricotta until well combined.

4. In a medium bowl, use a handheld mixer on medium speed to beat the egg whites to soft peaks.

5. Using a large flexible spatula, fold the egg whites into the ricotta just to combine.

6. Fold in the lemon zest or rum.

finale TO ASSEMBLE AND SERVE

1. Divide the ricotta filling evenly between the prepared crusts.

2. Decoratively arrange the dough strips on top of the filling. Lay strips from left to right and top to bottom in a crisscross pattern.

3. Fold over the excess dough so that it just covers the edges of the strips, trimming if necessary. You may also have to trim the pastry strips.

4. If using sanding sugar, brush the pastry with the egg wash and sprinkle the sanding sugar over the pastry. (The egg wash is not necessary if you are not using the sanding sugar.)

5. Bake the cakes until golden and a cake tester inserted into the centers comes out clean, 50 to 60 minutes, rotating the pans halfway through. Do not open the oven door during the first 15 minutes of baking.

6. Transfer the pans to a wire rack and allow the cakes to cool completely, then carefully remove them from the pans and transfer to cake plates or stands.

7. If you didn't use sanding sugar, to serve, dust the cakes with confectioners' sugar. Garnish with fresh fruit.

8. Store in an airtight container in the refrigerator for up to 1 week and in the freezer for up to 3 months.

Abruzzo Sweet Cheesecake

Cheesecake with Brandy-Cherry Sauce

Torta al Formaggio con Salsa di Ciliegie al Brandy

MAKES 1 (9-INCH) CHEESECAKE

Cheesecake with Brandy-Cherry Sauce

Cheesecakes taste best at room temperature, but it's much easier to slice while it's cold. When I'm hosting a dinner party, I remove the cheesecake from the refrigerator, cut my serving slices, and plate. Then I prepare a pot of coffee or espresso, sometimes both, and put it on the stovetop to brew (my family and friends prefer percolated coffee, as do I). I then prepare my after-dinner liqueurs. And when the coffee is finished brewing after about twenty minutes, the cheesecake has almost come to room temperature. By the time I bring the coffee, liqueurs, and cheesecake to the table, the cheesecake is the right temperature.

uno CROSTA DI BISCOTTI (GRAHAM CRACKER CRUST)

2¼ cups (270 g) graham cracker crumbs

¼ cup (57 g) superfine sugar

½ cup (113 g) unsalted butter, melted

due RIPIENO DI FORMAGGIO (CREAM CHEESE FILLING)

5¼ cups (1.26 kg) cream cheese, softened

1⅔ cups (375 g) superfine sugar

3 tablespoons (24 g) all-purpose flour, sifted

finely grated zest of ½ lemon

finely grated zest of ½ orange

1 teaspoon pure vanilla extract

5 large eggs, at room temperature

2 large egg yolks, at room temperature

tre SALSA DI CILIEGIE AL BRANDY (BRANDY-CHERRY TOPPING)

1½ tablespoons (14 g) cornstarch

3 tablespoons (45 ml) water

4⅔ cups frozen or 5 cups fresh sweet cherries, pitted, divided

½ cup (120 ml) orange juice

¼ cup (57 g) superfine sugar

finely grated zest of ½ lemon

splash of freshly squeezed lemon juice

finely grated zest of ½ orange

2 tablespoons (30 ml) brandy

CAKES AND CHEESECAKES **49**

uno TO MAKE THE GRAHAM CRACKER CRUST

1. Position a rack in the center of the oven. Preheat the oven to 350°F (180°C). Unlatch a 9-inch springform pan, flip the base over so the lip is on the underside, and cover the base with a sheet of parchment paper, leaving a 1½-inch overhang. Reassemble the pan. Using a pastry brush, coat the paper and sides of the pan with softened butter.

2. In a medium bowl, stir together the graham cracker crumbs and sugar. Add the melted butter and stir until the mixture is evenly moistened.

3. Press the crumb mixture onto the bottom and up the sides of the prepared pan, stopping about 1 inch from the top of the pan.

4. Preheat the oven to 500°F (260°C) and chill the pan in the freezer while you prepare the cream cheese filling.

due TO MAKE THE CREAM CHEESE FILLING

1. In a stand mixer fitted with the paddle attachment, beat the cream cheese on medium speed until smooth, about 2 minutes, scraping down the sides and bottom of the bowl and the paddle, as needed.

2. Reduce the speed to low and gradually add the sugar and flour. Beat until smooth, about 2 minutes (do not overmix).

3. Add the lemon zest, orange zest, and vanilla. Beat to just combine.

4. Reduce the speed to low and add the eggs and egg yolks one at a time, beating to just combine after each addition, about 30 seconds (do not overmix), scraping the sides and bottom of the bowl after each addition.

TO ASSEMBLE

1. Remove the crust from the freezer. Set the pan in the center of a rimmed baking sheet to catch any drips while the cake bakes.

2. Pour the filling through a fine-mesh sieve (to catch any lumps) into the crust, using an offset spatula to level the filling.

3. Bake until puffed, about 12 minutes. Pay close attention—some ovens will brown the top quicker than others. I place a sheet of parchment over the top of the springform pan when the cheesecake top has just set, about the 6-minute mark for me.

4. Reduce the oven temperature to 200°F (95°C) and continue baking until the cheesecake is mostly firm but the center still has a slight jiggle when the pan is gently shaken, about 1 hour.

5. Transfer the pan to a wire rack. Run a sharp, thin knife around the top edge of the cheesecake to loosen it to prevent the surface from cracking as it cools. Cool completely in the pan on the wire

Torta Sette Strati

Seven-Layer Cake

This *torta* requires planning ahead. If I'm making this *torta* for a dinner party, I usually begin the preparations three or four days in advance, and two days in advance I begin the assembly. If this is your first time making a cake like this, don't stress about the uniformity of the layers, because when you serve your guests their slices, it's the last thing they will be thinking about. They'll be too busy trying to figure out how they can get another dinner invite! It's a dessert people will definitely be talking about at the office water cooler on Monday morning. To make this *torta*, you'll need a 9 x 4-inch mousse ring or a 9-inch springform pan that is at least 4-inches deep.

Feuilletine is a European cookie crunch made of thin, crispy, buttery flakes. It's traditionally used to give a crunchy texture to ganache, fine chocolates, pastries, and cakes. I've found it available only through professional baking suppliers, but there are wonderful substitutions. In this recipe, I like the Pirouline brand wafer cookies because they are available with a hazelnut cream filling, which enhances the hazelnut in this *torta*, but any wafer cookies will do. Gavottes Crêpes Dentelles from France are another delicious substitution. However, easier to find are corn flakes, Rice Krispies, and wafer sugar cones, which will all work well in this recipe.

uno TORTA GENOVESE (GENOISE SPONGE CAKE)

3½ tablespoons (50 g) unsalted butter

8 large eggs, at room temperature

1 cup plus 5¼ teaspoons (250 g) superfine sugar

1 vanilla bean, split and seeded

2 cups (250 g) 00 (doppio zero) flour or all-purpose flour

pinch of salt

due DISCO DI PRALINATO AL CIOCCOLATO (CHOCOLATE PRALINE DISK)

1¾ ounces (50 g) good-quality milk chocolate

1¾ ounces (50 g) good-quality white chocolate

2 tablespoons (25 g) unsalted butter

4 tablespoons (76 g) Hazelnut Praline Paste (page 21)

1¾ ounces (50 g) feuilletine or wafer cookies, coarsely chopped (about 7 or 8 cookies) (see sidebar)

tre MOUSSE AL CIOCCOLATO AL LATTE E NOCCIOLE (MILK CHOCOLATE–HAZELNUT MOUSSE)

1½ cups (355 g) cold heavy cream

8 ounces (226 g) good-quality milk chocolate, finely chopped

3 tablespoons (42 g) superfine sugar

2 tablespoons (30 ml) water

4 large egg yolks

3 tablespoons (57 g) Hazelnut Praline Paste (page 21)

1 teaspoon pure vanilla extract

pinch of salt

quattro BAGNA AL LIQUORE FRANGELICO (FRANGELICO SIMPLE SYRUP)
Prepare the syrup about one-half hour prior to assembling the cake.

½ cup (120 ml) water

½ cup (113 g) superfine sugar

¼ cup (60 ml) Frangelico

cinque MOUSSE AL CIOCCOLATO (CHOCOLATE MOUSSE)
Prepare the mousse on the day you assemble the cake.

3 cups (710 ml) cold heavy cream

16 ounces (454 g) good-quality bittersweet chocolate, 60%, finely chopped

¼ cup plus 2 tablespoons (85 g) superfine sugar

3 tablespoons (45 ml) water

8 large egg yolks

2 teaspoons pure vanilla extract

pinch of salt

sei NOCCIOLE CARAMELLATE (CARAMELIZED HAZELNUTS)
Prepare caramelized hazelnuts on the day you serve the cake.

24 hazelnuts, toasted and skinned (see page 20)

1½ cups (338 g) superfine sugar

¼ cup plus 2 tablespoons (90 ml) water

sette GLASSATA AL CIOCCOLATO (CHOCOLATE GLAZE)
Prepare the glaze on the day you serve the cake. For best results, once the glaze has cooled immediately pour on the frozen cake.

1 cup plus 3 tablespoons (280 ml) heavy cream

5 ounces (140 g) good-quality dark chocolate, 70%, finely chopped

5 ounces (140 g) good-quality milk chocolate, finely chopped

⅔ cup (140 g) superfine sugar (see note)

¾ cup (170 g) unsalted butter, cut into 12 (1-tablespoon) pieces, at room temperature

uno TO MAKE THE GENOISE SPONGE CAKES

1. Preheat the oven to 350°F (180°C). Using a large pastry brush, butter 2 (8-inch) round cake pans. Line the bottoms with parchment paper rounds, butter the paper, and dust the bottoms and sides with flour, tapping out any excess.

2. Melt the butter in a small saucepan over low heat, occasionally swirling the pan over the burner, about 5 minutes (to bring out the nutty flavor). Remove from the heat and set aside to cool.

3. Place the eggs, sugar, and vanilla seeds (reserve the bean for another use) in the bowl of a stand mixer. Place the bowl over a saucepan of simmering water, and using a large balloon whisk, beat constantly until the mixture is hot to the touch, about 5 minutes.

4. Remove the bowl from the heat and attach to a stand mixer fitted with the whip attachment. Beat at high speed until the mixture has doubled in volume and has reached the ribbon stage (when the whip is lifted, the mixture should fall back into the bowl in a ribbon), about 10 minutes.

5. Using a fine-mesh sieve, sift one-third of the flour into the egg mixture and gently fold in with a large flexible spatula. Sift and then gently fold in one-half of the remaining flour just to combine (do not overmix).

6. Stir the salt into the cooled butter. Sift the remaining flour into the egg mixture, then gently fold it in along with the salted butter just to combine (do not overmix the batter or the cake won't rise well).

7. Divide the batter evenly between the prepared pans.

8. Bake until a cake tester inserted into the center of a cake comes out clean, about 30 minutes, rotating the pans halfway through.

9. Transfer the cakes to a wire rack to cool for 10 minutes. Remove the cakes from the pans and transfer directly to the wire rack to cool completely.

10. Once cooled, wrap one cake in plastic and place in an airtight container. Transfer to the freezer to store for later use. Wrap the remaining cake in plastic and transfer to the freezer to chill for 30 minutes. Remove from the freezer. If needed, use a large serrated knife to level the top of the cake, then cut it horizontally into two even layers. Store wrapped in plastic in the refrigerator or freezer until ready to assemble the *torta*.

due TO MAKE THE CHOCOLATE PRALINE DISKS

1. To make paper collars, cut 2 (27 x 3-inch) strips of acetate paper or parchment paper. Wrap one strip around the base of the sponge cake, keeping the bottom flush with the work surface. Secure the collar with tape, remove from the cake, and set aside. Repeat with the remaining collar. Place both collars on a baking sheet and place a sheet of plastic wrap inside each collar with a 2-inch overhang, smoothing out the plastic on the base and sides. Set aside.

2. In a medium bowl set over a pan of simmering water over low heat (do not let the bowl touch the water), combine the milk chocolate, white chocolate, butter, and praline paste, stirring until the chocolate and butter have melted and the mixture is well combined.

3. Remove from the heat. Stir in the chopped *feuilletine* or wafer cookies with a large flexible spatula.

4. Divide the mixture equally between the paper collars and spread evenly with a small offset spatula. Cover the disks with a large sheet of parchment paper and transfer to the freezer until firm, about 1 hour.

tre TO MAKE THE MILK CHOCOLATE–HAZELNUT MOUSSE

1. In a cold bowl, using a handheld mixer with cold beaters, beat the heavy cream at high speed to soft peaks. Transfer the whipped cream to an airtight container, cover, and refrigerate to chill.

2. In a heatproof bowl set over a saucepan of just-simmering water (do not let the bowl touch the water), melt the chocolate. Set aside and allow to cool slightly.

3. In a small saucepan, bring the sugar and water to a boil over high heat, stirring to dissolve the sugar. Attach a candy thermometer to the side of the saucepan and continue boiling the syrup, without stirring, until the syrup reaches 243°F (117°C), about 1 minute.

4. Meanwhile, in a medium bowl, use a handheld mixer to beat the egg yolks at high speed until pale in color and frothy.

5. When the syrup comes to temperature, reduce the mixer speed to low and continue to beat the egg yolks while carefully pouring the hot syrup in a steady stream down the side of the bowl, making sure the syrup does not touch the beaters. Increase the speed to high and continue to beat until thick, almost white in color, and cooled to a temperature of 85°F (29°C), about 5 minutes.

6. Beat in the hazelnut praline paste until well combined.

7. Whisk in the melted chocolate, vanilla, and salt.

8. Remove the whipped cream from the refrigerator. Whisk one-third into the chocolate mixture to combine well and to loosen the mixture. Using a large flexible spatula, fold in the remaining whipped cream in two additions.

9. Pass the mousse through a fine-mesh sieve into a large bowl (discard any solids).

10. Remove the firm praline disks from the freezer. Divide the mousse evenly between the molds, using an offset spatula to spread evenly.

11. Cover the molds with parchment paper and transfer to the freezer until firm, 4 to 6 hours.

quattro TO MAKE THE FRANGELICO SIMPLE SYRUP

1. Thirty minutes before assembling the cake, in a small saucepan, heat the water, sugar, and Frangelico over medium heat, stirring constantly, until the sugar is dissolved. Remove from the heat and set aside to cool.

cinque TO MAKE THE CHOCOLATE MOUSSE

1. In a cold bowl, using a handheld mixer with cold beaters, beat the heavy cream at high speed to soft peaks. Transfer the whipped cream to an airtight container, cover, and refrigerate to chill.

2. In a heatproof bowl set over a saucepan of just-simmering water (do not let the bowl touch the water), melt the chocolate. Set aside and allow to cool slightly.

3. In a small saucepan, bring the sugar and water to a boil over high heat, stirring to dissolve the sugar. Attach a candy thermometer to the side of the saucepan and continue boiling the syrup, without stirring, until the syrup reaches a temperature of 243°F (117°C), about 1 minute.

4. Meanwhile, in a medium bowl, use a handheld mixer to beat the egg yolks at high speed until pale in color and frothy.

5. When the syrup comes to temperature, reduce the mixer speed to low and continue to beat the egg yolks while carefully pouring the hot syrup in a steady stream down the side of the bowl, making sure the syrup does not touch the beaters. Increase the speed to high and continue to beat until the mixture is thick and almost white in color and has cooled to a temperature of 85°F (29°C), about 5 minutes.

6. Whisk in the melted chocolate, vanilla, and salt.

7. Remove the whipped cream from refrigerator. Whisk one-third into the chocolate mixture to combine well and to loosen the mixture. Using a large flexible spatula, fold in the remaining whipped cream in two additions.

8. Pass the mousse through a fine-mesh sieve into a large bowl (discard any solids).

TO ASSEMBLE THE CAKE

1. Line a rimmed baking sheet with parchment paper. Tear off an 18-inch sheet of plastic wrap and place it on the baking sheet over the parchment. Center a 9 x 4-inch ring mold on top of the plastic wrap. (If using a 9-inch springform pan for a mold, unlatch the ring and flip the base so the lip is facing down. Line the base with a sheet of parchment paper slightly larger than the base, attach the ring, and latch. Center the pan on the plastic on the baking sheet.) Line the sides of the mold with acetate paper or parchment paper, making sure the paper is the same height as your mold. Lift and wrap the plastic around the mold and secure it with tape or a rubber band.

2. Spoon two-thirds of the chocolate mousse into the mold. Using a flexible rubber spatula, spread the mousse to the edges of the mold and up the sides to the top, maintaining an even thickness all the way around. (The cake layers will be enclosed within the chocolate mousse; for best presentation, it's important to try to achieve the same thickness on the base and up the sides so when the cake is cut into slices, all the layers are uniform.)

3. Remove the genoise sponge cake disks and the chocolate praline–mousse disks from the freezer, making sure the mousse is firm. Working quickly, place a sheet of parchment paper on your work surface. Place one cake layer on the paper, brush with the Frangelico syrup, and place one chocolate praline–mousse disk on top of the cake. Add the second cake disk to the stack, brush with simple syrup, and top with the second praline-mousse disk. If the mousse has started to soften, place the stack in the freezer to firm up before proceeding.

4. Carefully place the stack into the mousse-filled mold, making sure the stack is centered.

5. Transfer the remaining chocolate mousse to the mold, filling the sides and creating a final layer of mousse on the top, flush with the top of the mold. Use an offset spatula to smooth out the mousse to the edges. Transfer to the freezer, uncovered. Once the top of the mousse is set, cover with plastic, and chill overnight.

DAY OF SERVING:

set TO MAKE THE CARAMELIZED HAZELNUTS

1. Prepare your work area prior to beginning the caramel-making process. Cut 24 pieces of tape, one to secure each skewer to the countertop after dipping the hazelnuts. (I stick the cut pieces of tape to the edge of the countertop, leaving a bit of an overhang for easy removal.) Spread newspaper directly below the work surface where you will be securing the skewers. To prepare an ice water bath, fill a large bowl half full with ice and cover the ice with cold water. Set aside.

2. Gently insert the pointed end of a long wooden skewer into the side of each hazelnut (it is much easier to insert the skewers when the hazelnuts are warm).

3. In a heavy medium saucepan over medium heat, bring the sugar and water to a boil, stirring until the sugar is dissolved and the syrup is clear.

4. Attach a candy thermometer to the side of the saucepan. Continue to cook the syrup over medium heat, without stirring, occasionally swirling the pan over the burner, until the syrup reaches a medium amber color (between 320°F and 350°F, 160°C and 180°C). Use a pastry brush dipped in water to wash down any crystals that form on the sides of the pan as the syrup cooks.

5. Remove from the heat and immediately plunge the saucepan into the ice water bath for 1 minute to stop the cooking. Let the caramel stand on the countertop until thickened, about 10 minutes. (Test for doneness by dipping a skewer in the caramel, then lifting it about 3 inches; the caramel is ready when a thick drip slowly forms and holds a string.)

6. Dip a skewered hazelnut into the caramel, allowing the excess caramel to drip back into the saucepan. When the dripping syrup becomes a thin string, secure the opposite end of the skewer to the countertop with tape. Repeat with the remaining hazelnuts, securing the skewers a few inches apart. (If the caramel begins to harden before all the hazelnuts have been dipped, return the saucepan to the stovetop and warm over low heat. Do not stir the caramel, but occasionally swirl the pan over the burner.)

7. Allow the dipped hazelnuts to cool until the caramel strings have hardened, about 5 minutes. Break each caramel string to the desired length (I like to have some longer than others for visual appeal). Carefully remove the skewers.

8. Candied hazelnuts can be stored in an airtight container at room temperature, but they are at their best on the day they are made, as the strings are fragile.

sette TO MAKE THE CHOCOLATE GLAZE

1. In a small saucepan, heat the cream over low heat. Add the dark chocolate and milk chocolate, and continue to cook over low heat, stirring constantly with a wooden spoon, until both chocolates are melted.

2. Add the sugar and continue to stir over low heat until the sugar is dissolved and the mixture is smooth, about 3 minutes.

3. Remove from the heat and allow to cool for 10 minutes.

4. Add the butter one piece at a time, making sure each piece is almost incorporated before adding the next.

5. Strain the glaze through a fine-mesh sieve into a pourable container (discard any solids; it's important to strain the glaze to make sure any bits of chocolate are removed).

6. If not using the glaze immediately, store in an airtight container in the refrigerator. Reheat to a temperature from 85°F to 95°F (30°C to 35°C), and immediately coat the frozen cake.

Note: Dark chocolate is not as sweet as bittersweet or semisweet, and it also contains a higher percentage of cocoa fats (70%). When making glazes, I always recommend that you add half the sugar, taste, and if you prefer the chocolate sweeter, add the remaining sugar a little at a time until you've reached the desired sweetness.

finale TO FINISH THE CAKE AND SERVE

1. Center the frozen cake on a cake board that is slightly smaller than the size of the cake. To remove the ring mold, heat the sides of the mold with a crème brûlée torch or hair dryer (do not hold the heat in one spot, but run the torch or dryer back and forth over the sides). Remove the mold and paper collar. For best presentation, if the sides of the cake are not smooth or if there are any holes in the mousse, dip an offset spatula in hot water, dry it with a clean kitchen towel, and run it along the surface of the mousse to smooth it out. You may have to dip the spatula in the hot water a few times depending on how smooth the surface is to begin with. Pop the cake back in the freezer, uncovered, to chill until the sides are firm again.

2. Remove the cake from the freezer. If a thin film of ice crystals has formed on the cake's surface, very carefully remove the film by placing the cake on a flat work surface, laying a sheet of paper towel on it, and pressing gently (be particularly careful if the towel is textured), and repeat on the sides of the cake.

3. Place a small bowl on a rimmed baking sheet. Carefully center the cake on top of the bowl. Begin pouring the chocolate glaze in the center of the cake, working your way to the edges, and allowing the excess to drip off the sides (do not stop pouring until you've covered the cake enough that it begins dripping down the sides).

4. Transfer the cake to the refrigerator to thaw the cake and set the glaze, at least 30 minutes.

5. To serve, remove the cake from the refrigerator, transfer to a cake stand or cake plate. Arrange the caramelized hazelnuts on top off the cake (be very careful handling the hazelnuts because the caramel is sticky and the strands easily break). Once you place a hazelnut onto the cake it's best not to move it again because it will leave an indentation in the chocolate. I prefer to cut a parchment round and position my hazelnuts on that first, this way if I don't like how it looks I can easily change without ruining the top of the cake. I find it best to place one hazelnut in the center and use it as my starting point. For visual appeal try to vary the heights of the candied hazelnuts.

Mini Desserts

Chocolate and Cherry Cake

Torta al Cioccolato e Ciliega

MAKES 8 (3 X 3-INCH) CAKES

Chocolate and Cherry Cake

If you a have leftover batter after filling the mini cake pans for this recipe, use it to fill buttered mini muffin tins. Bake at 350°F (180°C) for 12 minutes. They make a perfect afternoon treat with coffee.

uno CAKE

unsweetened cocoa, for dusting the tins

1 cup (100 g) almond meal

½ cup plus 1½ tablespoons (75 g) all-purpose flour

½ package (8 g) lievito vaniglinato (yeast for cake with vanilla) (see page 8)

2¾ cups (400 g) cherries, divided (about 50 large cherries)

½ cup (113 g) unsalted butter, cut into 8 equal pieces, plus more for the pan

8 ounces (226 g) good-quality bittersweet chocolate, 60%, finely chopped

3 tablespoons (45 ml) strongly brewed coffee

1 vanilla bean, seeded, or 1 teaspoon pure vanilla extract

2 tablespoons (30 ml) Grand Marnier

¾ cup plus 1 tablespoon (185 g) superfine sugar, divided

5 large eggs, separated, at room temperature

finale ASSEMBLY

10 ounces (285 g) good-quality semisweet chocolate, finely chopped

Bubble Sugar, for garnish (recipe follows)

uno TO MAKE THE CAKE

1. Preheat the oven to 350°F (180°C). Butter 8 (3-inch) cake pans and dust with cocoa, tapping out any excess. Arrange the pans on a rimmed baking sheet.

2. Using a fine-mesh sieve, sift the almond meal, all-purpose flour, and *lievito vaniglinato* into a small bowl. Whisk to combine well. Set aside.

3. Stem, pit, and finely chop half the cherries and set aside. For the remaining cherries that will be used for garnish, pit, but keep the stem intact.

4. Place the butter and chocolate in a heatproof bowl and set over a pan of just-simmering water (do not let the bowl touch the water). Stir until the mixture is smooth and the chocolate and butter have melted. Remove the bowl from the pan. Stir in the coffee, vanilla extract, if using, and Grand Marnier. Set aside to cool slightly.

5. Set aside 3 tablespoons of the sugar. In a medium bowl, use a handheld mixer to beat the egg yolks at medium speed, gradually adding the remaining sugar until pale in color, 2 to 3 minutes. Add the vanilla seeds, if using, and beat to just combine.

6. Add the chocolate mixture and beat to just combine.

7. Using a large flexible spatula, fold in the flour mixture. Fold in the chopped cherries.

8. In a stand mixer fitted with the whip attachment, beat the egg whites, beginning on low speed and gradually increasing to high. When the egg whites reach soft peaks, gradually stream in the reserved 3 tablespoons sugar and continue beating to stiff peaks.

9. Using a large flexible spatula, add the whipped egg whites to the batter in three additions.

10. Divide the batter evenly among the prepared pans, filling each a little more than half full. Bake until a cake tester inserted into the center comes out clean, 18 to 22 minutes.

11. Transfer the pans to a wire rack to cool for 3 to 4 minutes. Remove the cakes from the pans and return directly to the wire rack to cool completely.

finale TO ASSEMBLE AND SERVE

1. To make chocolate ribbons to decorate the cakes, prepare a template using a strip of acetate or parchment paper. Use a measuring tape to determine the height of the cake and the distance around it. Cut the strip of paper using your measurements. Wrap the paper template around each cake to ensure it is the appropriate size, making sure the strip is high enough to cover each cake and long enough to wrap all the way around. Make adjustments as needed.

2. Using your template, cut 8 strips of acetate paper. Set aside.

3. Line a baking sheet large enough to accommodate all the cakes with a few inches of space between each one with parchment paper or a silicone baking mat.

4. Melt the chocolate in a heatproof bowl set over a pan of just-simmering water (do not let the bowl touch the water). Stir until smooth, remove from the pan, and cool slightly.

5. Make sure the cakes are completely cool, and prepare one ribbon at a time. Lay one acetate strip on a flat surface. Using an offset spatula, spread chocolate evenly over the entire surface of the paper. Use the tip of a sharp paring knife to carefully lift the strip by slipping the tip under one corner. Working quickly but carefully, wrap the strip (chocolate-side toward the cake) around one cake (it will overlap slightly). Lightly press the strip into the side of the cake; the chocolate should be sticky. Use a strip of tape to secure the acetate strip to prevent it from unraveling. Repeat with the remaining strips.

6. Cover the cakes with a single sheet of parchment paper, and refrigerate to set the chocolate ribbons, about 2 hours.

7. To serve, transfer each cake to a dessert dish. Carefully, with the tip of a sharp paring knife, cut the tape and unwrap the acetate strip from each cake. Garnish each cake with 3 of the remaining whole stemmed cherries and shard of bubble sugar. For extra decoration, tie a ribbon around the middle of the cake.

Bubble Sugar

Bubble sugar is a simple way to dress up a variety of plated desserts, cakes, or cupcakes. To color the bubble sugar, add a few drops of food coloring just as the syrup comes to temperature. For a swirled look, stir a couple of times; for a solid color, stir until fully incorporated; and for a random design, swirl the pan once when you add the drops and let the bubbles do the work.

¾ cup (180 g) superfine sugar

⅓ cup plus 1 tablespoon (95 ml) water

2 tablespoons (30 ml) corn syrup or liquid glucose

2 tablespoons (30 ml) clear alcohol (like vodka, white rum, gin, or dry vermouth)

1. In a small saucepan over medium-high heat, bring the sugar, water, and corn syrup or glucose to a boil, stirring constantly until the sugar dissolves.

2. Stop stirring, attach a candy thermometer to the saucepan, and continue to cook to 315°F (160°C), occasionally brushing down the sides of the pan with a pastry brush dipped in water.

3. Meanwhile, crumple a sheet of parchment paper between your hands, then smooth out it out some, but not too much. The wrinkles will give the bubble sugar its texture. Lay the paper on a rimmed baking sheet.

4. Just before the sugar reaches the correct temperature, pour the alcohol on the parchment paper and use your hands to spread and coat the paper evenly.

5. When the sugar syrup comes to temperature, remove the pan from the heat and remove the thermometer. Tilt the baking sheet at a slight angle and carefully pour the sugar syrup on the top of the sheet so it runs down. Tilt the baking sheet from side to side to coat the paper. The alcohol will make the sugar bubble. Set the baking sheet on a wire rack to cool and completely set the bubble sugar.

6. Carefully peel the parchment paper from the back of the bubble sugar. Break into pieces and use to garnish your sweet treats.

7. Store unused bubble sugar in an airtight container at room temperature; it will keep for a few days.

Piccoli Torte Bavarese al Cioccolato e Vaniglia

Mini Chocolate and Vanilla Bavarian Cakes

To make these mini cakes, you'll need 12 (3 x 2-inch) ring molds, but it can also be made in 12 (6-ounce) ramekins. Pour ½ inch of batter into each ramekin and bake at 350°F (180°C) for about 8 minutes. Allow to cool completely on a wire rack, and trim the cakes to ½-inch high. Wrap each cake with a 4-inch paper collar and proceed with recipe.

uno TORTA AL CIOCCOLATO E MANDORLE (CHOCOLATE-ALMOND CAKE)

¾ cup plus 2 tablespoons (200 g) unsalted butter, cut into 18 pieces

¼ cup (30 g) unsweetened cocoa

½ cup (60 g) all-purpose flour

½ teaspoon baking powder

pinch of salt

1¼ cups (125 g) almond meal (finely ground almonds)

1 cup (225 g) superfine sugar

5 large egg whites, at room temperature

1 teaspoon pure vanilla extract

due BAVARESE AL CIOCCOLATO (CHOCOLATE BAVARIAN CREAM)

4 sheets (8 g) unflavored gold gelatin sheets

1¼ cups (300 ml) whole milk

1 vanilla bean, split and seeded

3 large egg yolks

¼ cup plus 3 tablespoons (100 g) superfine sugar

3½ ounces (100 g) good-quality bittersweet chocolate, finely chopped

1⅓ cups (325 ml) heavy cream

tre BAVARESE ALLA VANIGLIA (VANILLA BAVARIAN CREAM)

3 sheets (5 g) unflavored gold gelatin sheets

1 cup plus 1 tablespoon (250 ml) whole milk

1 vanilla bean, split and seeded

3 large egg yolks

¼ cup (57 g) superfine sugar

¾ cup plus 1½ tablespoons (200 ml) heavy cream

quattro GLASSA AL CIOCCOLATO (CHOCOLATE GLAZE)

> 4 ounces (113 g) good-quality bittersweet, 60%, or semisweet chocolate, finely chopped
>
> 4 ounces (113 g) heavy cream
>
> 1 tablespoon dark corn syrup
>
> 1 tablespoon (15 g) unsalted butter, cut into 4 pieces, at room temperature

finale ASSEMBLY

> Sweetened Whipped Cream (page 13)
>
> grated chocolate, for dusting

uno TO MAKE THE CHOCOLATE-ALMOND CAKE

1. Preheat the oven to 350°F (180°C). Line a 13 x 18-inch rimmed baking sheet with parchment paper or a silicone baking mat. If using parchment paper, lightly coat the paper with cooking spray or butter—do not coat the sides of the pan—and make sure the paper is cut to fit inside the pan, not covering the sides.

2. In a small saucepan over medium-low heat, melt the butter, occasionally swirling the pan over the burner, until it begins to brown and smells nutty, about 5 minutes. Watch the butter carefully at the 3-minute mark; once butter begins to brown, it turns quickly and it can easily burn. Remove from the heat and set aside to cool.

3. Using a fine-mesh sieve, sift the cocoa two times onto a sheet of parchment paper, then sift together the cocoa, flour, baking powder, and salt into a large bowl. Add the almond meal and sugar, and whisk to combine well.

4. Add the egg whites one at a time, whisking to just combine after each addition (do not overmix).

5. Stir the vanilla into the cooled butter, then add the butter to the batter in a steady stream, whisking to just combine.

6. Pour the batter onto the prepared baking sheet, spreading it evenly with an offset spatula.

7. Bake until a cake tester inserted into the center comes out clean, 15 to 18 minutes. Transfer the baking sheet to a wire rack and allow the cake to cool completely in the pan.

8. Place a sheet of parchment paper on top of the cooled cake. Fit a second rimmed baking sheet on top of the parchment and flip the cake over so that it rests on the back of the second sheet. Carefully remove the parchment paper or silicone baking mat from the cake. Grab the corners of the paper or mat and carefully transfer the cake back to the wire rack.

9. Wrap the cake in plastic wrap and transfer to the freezer for at least 30 minutes. The cake is extremely moist, and freezing it makes assembling the mini cakes much easier.

10. Remove the cold cake from the freezer. Using a 3 x 2-inch ring mold or a 3-inch round cookie cutter, cut 12 cake rounds.

11. Arrange the ring molds on a rimmed baking sheet lined with parchment paper or a silicone baking mat. Line the sides of the ring molds with acetate paper or parchment paper, making sure the paper is 1 inch higher than the mold.

12. Place one cake round into each mold, cover, and transfer to the refrigerator to chill.

due TO MAKE THE CHOCOLATE BAVARIAN CREAM

1. Soak the gelatin sheets in cold water until softened, 15 minutes. To prepare an ice water bath, fill a large bowl half full with ice and cover the ice with cold water. Set aside.

2. In a small saucepan over medium heat, bring the milk and the vanilla bean and seeds just to a boil. Remove from the heat, cover, and let steep for 3 minutes.

3. Meanwhile, in a large bowl, use a large whisk to beat together the egg yolks and sugar until thick and pale in color.

4. Gradually, add the hot milk mixture to the egg mixture in a steady stream, whisking constantly until well combined.

5. Return the mixture to the saucepan and cook over low heat until thickened and it reaches a temperature from 175°F to 180°F (80°C to 82°C), making sure the mixture doesn't boil.

6. Remove from the heat. Add the chocolate and stir until melted.

7. Remove the gelatin sheets from the water, squeeze out any excess liquid, and add to the chocolate-milk mixture, stirring until dissolved.

8. Strain the mixture through a fine-mesh sieve into a medium heatproof bowl (discard the solids). Place the bowl over the ice water bath, stirring occasionally until cool.

9. In a large bowl, use a handheld mixer to beat the heavy cream to soft peaks.

10. Fold the whipped cream into the cooled milk mixture in two additions. Strain the cream through a fine-mesh sieve once more, if desired.

11. Divide the chocolate cream evenly among the cake molds. Cover with plastic and refrigerate until set, 3 to 4 hours

12. When the chocolate cream is almost set, prepare the vanilla cream.

tre TO MAKE THE VANILLA BAVARIAN CREAM

1. Follow the same instructions as for the chocolate Bavarian cream with two exceptions: Steep the vanilla bean and seeds for 15 to 20 minutes. And of course, no chocolate is added.

2. When the chocolate cream is set, divide the vanilla cream evenly among the ring molds. Cover with plastic and refrigerate until set, 3 to 4 hours, or preferably overnight.

3. When the vanilla cream is set and you are ready to serve, prepare the chocolate glaze.

quattro TO MAKE THE CHOCOLATE GLAZE

1. Place the chocolate in a medium heatproof bowl.

2. In a small saucepan, heat the heavy cream and corn syrup over low heat until the corn syrup dissolves and small bubbles just begin to form around the sides of the pan.

3. Pour the cream mixture over the chocolate, making sure the chocolate is completely covered. Set aside for 2 minutes.

4. Using a small flexible spatula, beginning in the center of the bowl and working your way to the edges, stir until the chocolate is smooth. Add the butter, one piece at a time, whisking to combine well.

5. Immediately pour the glaze through a fine-mesh sieve into a small pourable container. This will ensure the glaze is smooth by catching any small bits of chocolate.

finale TO ASSEMBLE

1. To serve, remove the ring molds or ramekins and unwrap the acetate or parchment paper. Transfer the cakes to individual dessert dishes.

2. Spoon chocolate glaze over the tops of the cakes. Pipe or spoon whipped cream onto the cakes and dust with grated chocolate.

Mini Chocolate and Vanilla Bavarian Cakes

Pear and Chocolate Cake

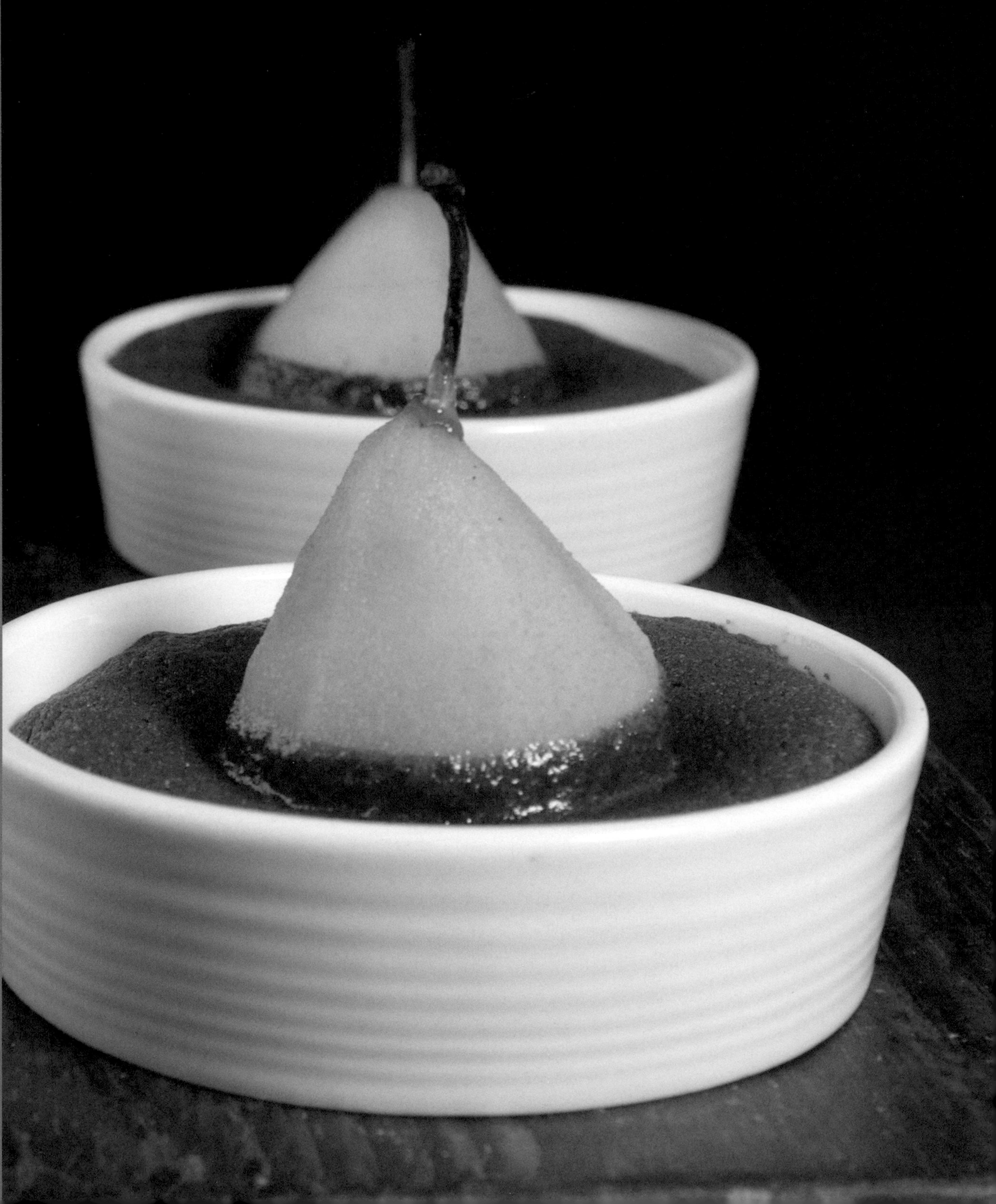

Torta di Pere e Cioccolato

Pear and Chocolate Cake

This Italian classic features one of my favorite combinations: pear and chocolate. This cake is typically made with crispy amaretti cookies, which gives it a rich almond flavor. It's very important to choose pears that are ripe but firm. Prior to baking the cakes, the pears are poached in simple syrup flavored with white wine, cinnamon, and vanilla, which gives them a delectable flavor.

uno POACHED PEARS

3 cups (830 ml) water

1 cup (240 ml) sweet white wine (like Riesling)

1⅓ cups (300 g) superfine sugar

8 small pears (like Forelle), firm but ripe

1 vanilla bean, split and seeded

1 cinnamon stick

due CHOCOLATE CAKE

3 large eggs

3½ ounces (100 g) amaretti cookies, finely ground (about 35 cookies)

¼ cup (31 g) all-purpose flour

4 ounces (113 g) good-quality dark chocolate, 70%, finely chopped

1 tablespoon liqueur (like Grand Marnier, pear brandy, calvados, or kirsch)

1 teaspoon pure vanilla extract

⅓ cup plus 1½ tablespoons (100 ml) whole milk

½ cup plus 1 tablespoon (125 g) unsalted butter, at room temperature

⅔ cup (150 g) superfine sugar, divided

1½ ounces (40 g) good-quality semisweet chocolate, cut into 8 strips (optional)

uno TO MAKE THE POACHED PEARS

1. Make a cartouche from a piece of parchment paper (see sidebar on page 76).

2. In a medium saucepan over medium heat, bring the water, wine, and sugar to a boil, stirring until the sugar dissolves.

3. Meanwhile, carefully core and peel the pears, keeping their shape and stems intact.

4. Add the vanilla bean and seeds and the cinnamon stick to the poaching liquid. Reduce the heat to low and gently simmer.

5. Add the pears to the poaching liquid and cover with the cartouche. Cook until tender, 20 to 25 minutes.

6. Remove the cartouche and the pears from poaching liquid and set aside to cool.

7. To make a sauce to serve with cakes, increase the heat to high and reduce the syrup to about 1 cup, 30 to 35 minutes.

due TO MAKE THE CHOCOLATE CAKE

1. Separate the eggs. Place the yolks in a small bowl and the whites in a stand mixer. Cover each bowl with plastic wrap and allow the eggs to come to room temperature, about 30 minutes.

2. Preheat the oven to 350°F (180°C). Line a rimmed baking sheet with parchment paper and place 8 (4½–inch) ovenproof dishes on top.

3. Using a fine-mesh sieve, sift together the amaretti cookies and flour onto a sheet of parchment paper. Set aside.

4. Melt the chocolate in a heatproof bowl set over a pan of just-simmering water (do not let the bowl touch the water), stirring occasionally until smooth. Remove the bowl from the pan and set aside to cool slightly. Stir in the liqueur, vanilla, and milk.

5. Reserve 3 tablespoons of the sugar. In a large bowl, use a handheld mixer to cream the butter and the remaining sugar at high speed until fluffy and pale in color.

6. Add the egg yolks one at a time, beating well and scraping the sides and bottom of the bowl after each addition.

7. Add the chocolate mixture to the egg yolk mixture, beating to combine well and scraping down the sides and bottom of the bowl as needed.

8. In a stand mixer fitted with the whip attachment, beat the egg whites, beginning on low speed and gradually increasing to high. When the egg whites reach soft peaks, gradually stream in the reserved 3 tablespoons sugar and continue beating to stiff peaks.

9. Using a large flexible spatula, fold the egg whites into the batter in three additions.

10. Spoon the batter evenly among the baking dishes, filling each half full. If using semisweet chocolate strips, place a strip in each hollowed poached pear. Place one poached pear in the center of each cake, gently pressing until the pear touches the bottom of the baking dish.

11. Bake until a cake tester inserted into the center of a cake comes out clean, 18 to 22 minutes, rotating the baking sheet halfway through.

12. To serve, drizzle each cake with the reduced poaching liquid, if desired.

HOW TO MAKE A CARTOUCHE

A cartouche is a circle of parchment paper with a hole in the center cut to fit the inside of a saucepan. To make one, cut a square of parchment paper slightly larger than your saucepan. Fold the square in half, then in half again, and then fold it diagonally to make a triangle. Position the point of the triangle in the center of the saucepan and rest the opposite end on the rim. Cut the paper at the rim, cut the point to make a hole in the center, then unfold the cartouche.

Piccoli Torta alla Vaniglia con Crema di Ricotta, Panna Montata al Cacao e Marsala

Cannoli Cupcakes with Marsala-Chocolate Whipped Cream

If you're decorating the cupcakes with mini cannoli, be sure to fill the cannoli just before serving to ensure the shells stay crispy. Unlike classic whipped cream, the marsala-chocolate whipped cream is made with gelatin, so it's firm enough to use as a frosting in this recipe.

uno PICCOLI TORTA ALLA VANIGLIA (VANILLA CUPCAKES)

1¾ cups (219 g) all-purpose flour

2 teaspoons baking powder

¼ teaspoon salt

¾ cup (170 g) unsalted butter, at room temperature

1¼ cups (281 g) superfine sugar

2 large eggs, at room temperature

2 large egg yolks, at room temperature

1½ teaspoons pure vanilla extract

1 cup (240 ml) whole milk

due CREMA DI RICOTTA (RICOTTA CREAM)

3½ cups Crema di Ricotta (Ricotta Cream) (page 14)

tre PANNA MONTATA AL CACAO E MARSALA (MARSALA-CHOCOLATE WHIPPED CREAM FROSTING)

2 tablespoons (15 g) unsweetened cocoa

¼ cup plus 2 tablespoons (47 g) confectioners' sugar

1 teaspoon unflavored powdered gelatin

2 tablespoons (30 ml) cold water

2 cups plus 2 tablespoons (500 ml) cold heavy cream

½ to 1 teaspoon sweet marsala, as needed

finale ASSEMBLY

24 Piccoli Cialde per Cannoli (Mini Cannoli Shells) (page 140) (optional)

confectioners' sugar, for dusting

uno TO MAKE THE VANILLA CUPCAKES

1. Preheat the oven to 350°F (180°C). Line 2 standard 12-cup muffins pans with paper liners. Set aside.

2. Using a fine-mesh sieve, sift the flour, baking powder, and salt onto a sheet of parchment paper.

3. In a stand mixer fitted with the paddle attachment, cream the butter and sugar at medium speed until light and fluffy, about 4 minutes.

4. Place the eggs and egg yolks in a liquid measuring cup. Add the vanilla and lightly beat with a fork. With the mixer running, gradually pour the egg mixture into the butter mixture, scraping down the sides and bottom of the bowl as needed.

5. Reduce the mixer speed to low. Add the flour mixture one-third at a time, alternating with adding the milk in two additions (beginning and ending with the flour mixture), beating to just combine after each addition.

6. Divide the batter evenly among the muffin cups, filling each one three-quarters full.

7. Bake the cupcakes, rotating the pans halfway through baking, until a cake tester inserted into the center of a cupcake comes out clean, about 20 minutes.

8. Transfer the pans to a wire rack to cool for a few minutes. Remove the cupcakes from the pans and transfer directly to the wire rack to cool completely. Transfer the cupcakes to an airtight container, and 30 minutes before assembly, place them in the freezer to chill (chilled cupcakes will be easier to hollow out).

due TO MAKE THE RICOTTA CREAM

1. Omit the candied citron and candied orange peel. If you'll be decorating the cupcakes with mini cannoli, before you add the chocolate chips, divide the cream between two bowls. Stir the chips into one bowl, and leave the second bowl plain. The plain filling is for the mini cannoli, because the chips will not pass through the small pastry tip, making it difficult to pipe the cream into the shells.

2. Transfer the filling to an airtight container and refrigerate until ready to use. The filling can be made one day in advance. Leftover ricotta cream can be stored in an airtight container in the refrigerator for up to 3 days.

tre FOR MARSALA-CHOCOLATE WHIPPED CREAM FROSTING

1. Using a fine-mesh sieve, sift the cocoa two times onto a sheet of parchment paper. Then sift the cocoa a third time with the confectioners' sugar into a small bowl and whisk to combine well.

2. Sprinkle the gelatin over the cold water in a small saucepan and allow to soften for 5 minutes. Place the saucepan over low heat and stir until the gelatin dissolves. Remove from the heat and let cool.

3. In a stand mixer fitted with the whip attachment, beat the heavy cream, cocoa mixture, and ½ teaspoon marsala on medium-high speed to barely a stiff peak. Taste, and add more marsala as needed.

4. With the mixer running, gradually pour the dissolved gelatin through a small fine-mesh sieve into the cream mixture, and continue to beat to stiff peaks.

5. Transfer the whipped cream to an airtight container and refrigerate until cold, 15 to 30 minutes.

finale TO ASSEMBLE AND SERVE

1. Using a sharp paring knife, cut a 1½-inch deep cone-shaped piece of cake from the center of each cupcake. Trim the cone piece into a round flat disk that will be used to seal the cupcake after filling with ricotta cream. Use a melon baller to hollow out the cupcake and make room for a little more filling.

2. Transfer the ricotta cream with chocolate chips to a large pastry bag fitted with a large plain tip. Working with one cupcake at a time, pipe ricotta cream into each hollowed out cupcake, filling almost to the top but leaving enough room for the disks of cake to sit flush with the top of the cupcake. Seal with the cake disks.

3. Transfer the marsala-chocolate whipped cream frosting to a large pastry bag fitted with a decorative tip (like a Wilton 1M). Pipe frosting onto the top of each cupcake.

4. If using mini cannoli, transfer the plain ricotta cream without chocolate chips to a small pastry bag fitted with a small plain tip (like a Wilton 18).

5. Working with one shell at a time, insert the pastry tip into one side of the cannoli shell, and gently squeeze (mini shells are very delicate) until the shell is half full. Repeat on the other end of the shell. Repeat with the remaining shells.

6. Top each cupcake with a mini cannoli and dust with confectioners' sugar.

7. Store cannoli cupcakes in an airtight container in the refrigerator. Bring to room temperature before serving.

Cannoli Cupcakes with Marsala-Chocolate Whipped Cream

Mini Lemon Mousse Cakes with Limoncello-Lemon Jelly

Mini Torte Mousse al Limone con Gelatina di Limone al Limoncello

Mini Lemon Mousse Cakes with Limoncello-Lemon Jelly

To make these mini cakes, you will need 6 (3 x 2-inch) ring molds. The sponge cake recipe makes 1 (13 x 18-inch) baking sheet, but you will need only half to make these mini cakes. Freeze the remaining cake for another use.

uno PAN DI SPAGNA ALLE MANDORLE E LIMONE (ALMOND-LEMON SPONGE CAKE)

8 ounces (227 g) almond paste

4 large eggs, at room temperature

¼ cup (31 g) all-purpose flour

¾ teaspoon baking powder

grated zest of 1 lemon

1 teaspoon pure vanilla extract

3 tablespoons (43 g) unsalted butter, melted and cooled

due BAGNA AL LIMONCELLO (LIMONCELLO SIMPLE SYRUP)

⅔ cup (150 g) sugar

½ cup (120 ml) water

2 (¾ inch) strips lemon zest

2 to 4 tablespoons (30 to 60 ml) limoncello

tre MOUSSE AL LIMONE (LEMON MOUSSE)

3½ sheets (6 g) gold gelatin sheets

1¼ cups (300 ml) whole milk

½ vanilla bean, split and seeded

3 large egg yolks plus 1 large egg white, at room temperature

½ cup plus 1 tablespoon (127 g) superfine sugar, divided

3 tablespoons plus ¾ teaspoon (30 g) cornstarch, sifted

grated zest of 1 lemon

½ cup (120 ml) freshly squeezed lemon juice (from 2 to 3 lemons)

2 tablespoons (30 ml) water

1 cup (240 ml) heavy cream

quattro GELATINA DI LIMONE AL LIMONCELLO (LIMONCELLO-LEMON JELLY)

　　4 sheets (6.6 g) gold gelatin sheets

　　¼ cup plus 2½ tablespoons (92 g) superfine sugar

　　1 cup (240 ml) water

　　zest from ½ lemon, cut into strips

　　¼ cup (60 ml) freshly squeezed lemon juice (from 1 to 2 lemons)

　　yellow food coloring, as needed

　　1 to 2 tablespoons (15 to 30 ml) limoncello

cinque FETTE DI LIMONE CANDITA (CANDIED LEMON SLICES)

　　1 lemon

　　1 cup (240 ml) water

　　1 cup (225 g) superfine sugar

finale ASSEMBLY

　　Sweetened Whipped Cream (page 13)

uno TO MAKE THE ALMOND-LEMON SPONGE CAKE

1. Preheat the oven to 350°F (180°C). Line a rimmed baking sheet with parchment paper or a silicone baking mat. If using parchment paper, butter the paper.

2. In a stand mixer fitted with the paddle attachment, beat the almond paste at medium speed until softened, 2 to 3 minutes.

3. Add the eggs one at a time, making sure each yolk is well incorporated before adding the next, until a smooth paste forms.

4. Replace the mixer's paddle attachment with the whip attachment. Beat at medium-high speed until thick and pale in color, 3 to 5 minutes.

5. Meanwhile, using a small fine-mesh sieve, sift the flour and baking powder together into a small bowl; whisk to combine well.

6. Add the lemon zest to the egg mixture, and beat to just combine. Reduce the mixer speed to low, add the flour mixture, and beat until just combined.

7. In a small bowl, stir the vanilla into the butter. With the mixer running at low speed, gradually add the butter to the egg mixture and beat to just combine.

8. Transfer the batter to the prepared baking sheet and use a large offset spatula to spread the batter evenly to the sides of the pan.

9. Bake until lightly golden, 18 to 22 minutes.

10. Transfer the baking sheet to a wire rack to cool for a few minutes. Then carefully remove the cake on the parchment paper or baking mat from the pan and set it on the wire rack to cool completely.

11. Once cooled, carefully the flip the cake by placing a sheet of parchment paper on top of the cake. Set the bottom of another baking sheet the same size on top of the parchment paper, and holding the baking sheet and wire rack securely, flip the cake onto the baking sheet. Peel off the parchment paper or silicone mat, wrap the cake in plastic wrap, and transfer to the freezer to chill until firm, 30 to 60 minutes.

due TO MAKE THE LIMONCELLO SIMPLE SYRUP

1. In a small saucepan over medium heat, bring the sugar, water, and lemon zest to a boil, stirring constantly until the sugar is dissolved. Remove from the heat and set aside to cool.

2. Strain the syrup through a fine-mesh sieve into a small bowl (discard the solids).

3. Stir the limoncello into the cooled syrup, and set aside.

4. Line a rimmed baking sheet with parchment paper or a silicone baking mat. Place 6 (3 x 2-inch) ring molds on top. Line the ring molds with acetate or parchment paper collars.

5. Remove the cake from the freezer and use one of the ring molds to cut 6 cake rounds. Brush the rounds with the limoncello simple syrup and place 1 cake round soaked-side up in the base of each ring mold. Transfer the baking sheet to the refrigerator until the syrup is set, 3 to 5 minutes. Leftover cake can be well wrapped in plastic and stored in the freezer for up to 1 month. It can be used for desserts like trifles and is also very handy to have around to make other mini layered cakes.

tre TO MAKE THE LEMON MOUSSE

1. Soak the gelatin sheets in a small bowl in very cold water until softened, 15 minutes.

2. Meanwhile, in a small saucepan over medium heat, bring the milk and the vanilla bean and seeds just to a boil. Remove from the heat, cover, and allow to steep, 10 to 12 minutes.

3. Reserve 2½ tablespoons sugar. In a medium bowl, using a large whisk, beat the egg yolks and the remaining sugar until pale in color. Add the cornstarch and beat until well combined (there should be no lumps).

4. Gradually add the hot milk mixture to the lightened egg yolks in a slow steady stream, whisking constantly, until well combined. Transfer the custard back to the saucepan.

5. Cook the custard over medium heat, stirring constantly, until thickened, 3 to 5 minutes.

6. Add the lemon zest and juice and cook over medium heat for 30 seconds. Remove from the heat.

7. Squeeze out the excess water from the softened gelatin sheets. Add the sheets to the custard, and stir to dissolve completely.

8. Strain the custard through a fine-mesh sieve into a small bowl (discard the solids). Place a sheet of plastic wrap directly on the surface of the custard to prevent a skin from forming. Set aside to cool.

9. Meanwhile, in a small saucepan, combine the reserved 2½ tablespoons sugar with the water. Place over medium heat and stir until the sugar is dissolved. Attach a candy thermometer to the side of saucepan and continue to cook the sugar, without stirring, to a temperature of 243°F (117°C).

10. Place the egg white in a small bowl, and when the sugar syrup reaches 230°F (110°C), begin beating the egg white with a handheld mixer at high speed.

11. When the syrup almost reaches 243°F (117°C), immediately remove from the heat (it will come up to temperature quickly off the heat). Reduce the mixer speed to low and gradually pour the syrup in a slow, steady stream down the side of the bowl into the egg white; make sure the syrup does not touch the beaters. Once the syrup is incorporated, increase the mixer speed to high and beat the egg white to stiff peaks.

12. Fold the whipped egg white into the slightly cooled custard in two additions. Place a sheet of plastic wrap directly on the surface of the custard mixture and refrigerate to cool completely.

13. Once the custard mixture is completely cool, in a small bowl, use a handheld mixer at high speed to beat the heavy cream to stiff peaks. Fold the whipped cream into the custard mixture one-third at a time.

14. Strain the mousse through a fine-mesh sieve into a large bowl (discard any solids).

15. Remove the cakes from the refrigerator. With a pastry bag or a spoon, evenly divide the lemon mousse among the ring molds. Use the back of a small spoon to level the tops of the mousse. Transfer the cakes to the refrigerator until set, 4 to 6 hours, or transfer to the freezer until firm, 2 to 3 hours. Do not proceed with the preparations for the limoncello-lemon jelly until the mousse layer is set.

quattro TO MAKE THE LIMONCELLO-LEMON JELLY

1. To prepare an ice water bath, fill a large bowl half full with ice and cover the ice with cold water. Set aside.

2. Soak the gelatin sheets in a small bowl in very cold water until softened, 15 minutes.

3. Meanwhile, in a small saucepan over medium heat, bring the sugar, water, and lemon zest and juice to a boil over medium heat, stirring constantly, until the sugar is dissolved. Remove from the heat.

4. Strain the mixture through a fine-mesh sieve into a small bowl.

5. Squeeze out the excess water from the softened gelatin sheets. Add the sheets to the lemon juice mixture and stir to dissolve completely.

6. Add the food coloring a few drops at a time until the desired color is achieved.

7. Stir in the limoncello to taste.

8. Place the bowl in the ice water bath and stir the jelly occasionally until thickened slightly, 5 to 7 minutes (do not cool too long or the jelly will begin to set).

9. Remove the cakes from the refrigerator or freezer. Pour the limoncello jelly over the mousse. Transfer the cakes to the refrigerator to set, 3 to 4 hours. Once the jelly is set, I like to transfer the cakes to the freezer for about 1 hour to firm up, making it much easier to remove the acetate or parchment collars. When the cakes are cold and firm, the collars unwrap easily without the mousse sticking to the paper.

cinque TO MAKE THE CANDIED LEMON SLICES

1. To prepare an ice water bath, fill a medium bowl half full with ice and cover the ice with cold water. Set aside. Line a rimmed baking sheet with parchment paper.

2. Wash and cut the lemon (do not remove the peel) into very thin slices with a sharp knife or a mandoline. Remove and discard the seeds.

3. Bring a medium saucepan of water to a rolling boil over high heat. Add the lemon slices and blanch until softened to help remove their bitterness, 1 to 2 minutes. Remove from the heat, drain the water, and immediately drop the lemon slices into the ice water bath. Drain and set aside.

4. In a medium skillet, bring the water and sugar to a boil over medium heat, stirring until the sugar is dissolved and the mixture is clear.

5. Reduce the heat to medium-low and add the lemon slices in a single layer. Simmer, uncovered, until translucent, about 1 hour.

6. Transfer the slices to the prepared baking sheet and allow to cool completely.

finale TO ASSEMBLE AND SERVE

1. When the cakes are set, remove from the refrigerator or freezer, remove the ring molds, and carefully unwrap the acetate or parchment paper. If the cakes were set in the freezer, transfer to the refrigerator to thaw before serving. If not serving immediately, store cakes in an airtight container in the refrigerator up to 3 days.

2. To serve, use an offset spatula to transfer the cakes to dessert plates, and garnish each one with a swirl of sweetened whipped cream and a candied lemon slice.

Millefoglie con Crema Pasticcera al Cioccolato Bianco e Lamponi Freschi

MAKES 6 (3-LAYER) OR 10 (2-LAYER) MILLE-FEUILLE

Raspberry and White Chocolate Mille-Feuille

Traditionally, *millefoglie* is prepared with three layers of *pasta sfoglia* (puff pastry) alternating with two layers of *crema pasticcera* (Italian pastry cream). It's either dusted with confectioners' sugar or topped with white and dark chocolate glaze. Today, the filling variations are endless.

uno PASTRY RECTANGLES

confectioners' sugar, for dusting

2 (10 x 10-inch) sheets (454 g) store-bought puff pastry, or Pasta Sfoglia (page 22)

due FILLING

3 cups Crema Pasticcera al Cioccolato Bianco (White Chocolate Pastry Cream) (page 11)

finale ASSEMBLY

fresh raspberries, for decorating

confectioners' sugar, for dusting

finely grated white chocolate, for decorating (optional)

uno TO MAKE THE PASTRY RECTANGLES

1. Line 2 rimmed baking sheets with parchment paper. Using a fine-mesh sieve, sift a light dusting of confectioners' sugar over the parchment paper.

2. Cut each pastry sheet into 10 (5 x 2-inch) rectangles, for a total of 20 rectangles. Use an offset spatula to transfer the rectangles to the prepared baking sheets (10 per sheet). Using a fine-mesh sieve, sift confectioners' sugar over the pastry. Transfer to the freezer to chill for 30 minutes.

3. Preheat the oven to 450°F (230°C). Remove 1 sheet of pastry rectangles from the freezer and dust again with confectioners' sugar. To prevent the dough from rising, top with a sheet of parchment paper, lay a second baking sheet on top, and weight it down with a ceramic baking dish. Reduce the oven to 375°F (190°C), and immediately transfer the pastry rectangles to the oven and bake until golden, 15 to 20 minutes.

4. Remove from the oven. Remove the ceramic baking dish, the top baking sheet, and the top parchment paper. Carefully flip the pastry rectangles over, return to the oven, and bake until golden and crisp, about 5 minutes longer.

5. Transfer the pastry rectangles to wire rack to cool. Return the oven to 450°F (230°C) and repeat with the remaining sheet of pastry rectangles, remembering to lower the temperature to 375°F (190°C) when ready to bake.

6. If not assembling the mille-feuille within 2 hours, transfer the cooled pastry rectangles to an airtight container and store at room temperature.

due TO MAKE THE FILLING

1. Strain the white chocolate pastry cream into a 9 x 13-inch baking dish (discard the solids). Using an offset spatula, spread the cream to the edges of the dish. Place a sheet of plastic wrap directly on the surface of the cream to prevent a skin from forming as it cools.

2. When the pastry cream is cool, if you find it has not thickened enough to hold a piped mound shape, refrigerate for about 30 minutes to thicken.

finale TO ASSEMBLE AND SERVE

1. Because the pastry dough can shrink while baking, even when it is weighted down, stack the pastry rectangles in groups of 3, and trim with a sharp knife as needed to make them the same size.

2. Transfer the pastry cream to a large pastry bag fitted with a large decorative tip (like a Wilton 1M).

3. Place 1 pastry rectangle on a clean work surface and pipe 2 rows of pastry cream on top (I usually pipe 2 rows of four 1-inch mounds, leaving a small space in between). Top with a second pastry rectangle. Repeat with another layer of pastry cream and a third pastry rectangle. Decorate with fresh raspberries.

4. Repeat with the remaining pastry rectangles and pastry cream.

5. Just before serving, lightly dust with confectioners' sugar and grated white chocolate, if using. Serve at room temperature.

Raspberry and White Chocolate Mille-Feuille

Piccoli Torta al Crema di Formaggio e Cioccolato Bianco con Composta di Mirtilli

Mini Blueberry–White Chocolate Cheesecakes

To make these minicakes, you'll need 8 (3 x 2-inch) ring molds. If you don't have the time to make the blueberry compote, this dessert is also lovely simply topped with fresh blueberries.

uno CROSTA DI BISCOTTO AMARETTI E MANDORLE (AMARETTI-ALMOND COOKIE CRUST)

  ½ cup (60 g) slivered almonds

  5 ounces (143 g) amaretti cookies (about 50 small cookies)

  ¼ cup (57 g) unsalted butter, melted

due RIPIENO DI CREMA AL FORMAGGIO E CIOCCOLATO BIANCO (WHITE CHOCOLATE CHEESECAKE FILLING)

  4 ounces (113 g) good-quality white chocolate, finely chopped

  1 cup plus 2 teaspoons (250 g) cream cheese, softened

  ½ cup plus 2 tablespoons (125 g) mascarpone cheese, softened

  ⅓ cup (75 g) superfine sugar

  2 large eggs

  1 teaspoon pure vanilla extract

tre COMPOSTA DI MIRTILLI (BLUEBERRY COMPOTE)

  ¼ cup (60 ml) freshly squeezed orange juice

  3 tablespoons (42 g) superfine sugar

  1 vanilla bean, split and seeded

  2 cups (296 g) fresh blueberries, divided

  ¾ teaspoon cornstarch

  1 tablespoon water

  ½ tablespoon grated orange zest

  1 teaspoon freshly squeezed lemon juice

  1 tablespoon liqueur, like crème de cassis, Grand Marnier, or kirsch

finale ASSEMBLY

  White Chocolate Curls (see page 171)

uno TO MAKE THE AMARETTI-ALMOND COOKIE CRUST

1. Line a rimmed baking sheet with parchment paper. Cut additional parchment paper into 8 (4¾-inch) squares. Cut heavy-duty aluminum foil into 16 (8-inch) squares. Stack two aluminum squares on top of each other. Top with one parchment square and then center a 3 x 2-inch ring mold on top. Gather up the foil and parchment squares and tightly wrap around the mold, making sure the base is smooth and flat. Using a small pastry brush, lightly butter the base and sides of the mold with softened unsalted butter. Transfer the mold to the prepared baking sheet. Wrapping the mold this way helps prevent water from seeping into the cheesecakes while baking. Take care to be sure there are no seams exposed halfway up the molds. Repeat with the 7 remaining ring molds.

2. In a food processor, process the almonds to a coarse crumb (if you would like a bit of crunch in the cookie crusts) or a fine crumb. Transfer to small bowl.

3. In the food processor, process the amaretti cookies to a fine crumb and add to the ground almonds.

4. Add the melted butter and stir to combine well until the crumbs are evenly moistened.

5. Divide the mixture evenly among the ring molds, about 2 tablespoons per mold. Using a tart tamper or the back of a small spoon, press the cookie mixture firmly and evenly into the base of each ring mold. Return the molds to the baking sheet, cover with plastic, and refrigerate until firm, about 30 minutes.

due TO MAKE THE WHITE CHOCOLATE CHEESECAKE FILLING

1. While the crusts refrigerate, place the white chocolate in a heatproof bowl set over a saucepan of just-simmering water over low heat (do not let the bowl touch the water), stirring occasionally, until the chocolate is melted and smooth. Set aside and allow to cool slightly.

2. In a stand mixer fitted with the paddle attachment, beat the cream cheese and mascarpone on medium speed until creamy and smooth (no lumps), 2 to 3 minutes.

3. Gradually add the sugar and continue to beat on medium speed until smooth, 1 to 2 minutes, scraping the sides and bottom of the bowl, and the paddle, as needed.

4. Add the eggs one at a time, beating just to combine after each addition, about 30 seconds. Scrape the sides and bottom of the bowl after each addition.

5. Add the melted white chocolate and the vanilla, and beat to just combine.

6. Remove the bowl from the mixer. Using a large flexible spatula, scrape the sides and bottom of the bowl and give the filling a quick stir. Strain through a fine-mesh sieve into a bowl to ensure a lump-free filling.

tre TO MAKE THE BLUEBERRY COMPOTE

1. In a small saucepan over low heat, bring the orange juice, sugar, the vanilla bean and seeds, and 1 cup of the blueberries to a simmer, stirring to dissolve the sugar. Cook until the berries are tender, about 4 minutes.

2. In a small bowl, dissolve the cornstarch in the water. Strain mixture through a small fine-mesh sieve into the blueberry mixture. Stir to combine well, and continue simmering until slightly thickened, about 2 minutes.

3. Add the remaining 1 cup blueberries and the orange zest and lemon juice, and cook for 1 minute longer.

4. Remove from the heat, stir in the liqueur, and remove the vanilla bean. Allow to cool completely.

5. If not using immediately, refrigerate in an airtight container. Bring to room temperature before serving.

quattro TO ASSEMBLE AND SERVE

1. Preheat the oven to 375°F (190°C). Bring a teakettle of water almost to a boil.

2. Remove the ring molds from the refrigerator and divide the cheesecake filling evenly among the crusts. To release any air bubbles, tap the molds on the countertop a couple of times.

3. Line a deep baking dish with a folded kitchen towel. Place the ring molds 1 to 2 inches apart in the dish on top of the towel (make sure the molds are still water tight).

4. Open the oven door and pull out the middle rack halfway; transfer the baking dish to the rack. Carefully fill the baking dish with enough hot water to come halfway up the sides of the molds, making sure no water gets in. Carefully push the baking dish into the center of the oven rack and then carefully push the oven rack back into the oven.

5. Bake until set around the edges with a slight wobble in the middle when the baking dish is gently shaken, 20 to 25 minutes, rotating the baking sheet about halfway through.

6. Carefully remove the baking dish from the oven and place on a flat, heatproof surface. Using tongs or a baking glove, quickly and carefully remove each mold and transfer to a wire rack (the cheesecakes will overbake if they are left in the hot water). Unwrap the molds but don't completely remove the paper until the cheesecakes have cooled completely. (Be careful when unwrapping; the molds are very hot.) Cool the cheesecakes completely on the rack.

7. Transfer the cooled cheesecakes to a baking sheet, cover loosely with plastic, and refrigerate overnight before unmolding.

8. To unmold, cut a cardboard round slightly smaller than the ring molds. Remove the cold cheesecakes from the refrigerator. Working with one cheesecake at a time, carefully run a knife around the edge. Place the cheesecake over the cardboard round, then place it on a glass that is slightly smaller than the mold. Carefully push the mold down and off the cake so the mold is around

the glass and the cake sits on top of the glass. Transfer the cheesecake from the cardboard to a serving dish. Repeat with the remaining cheesecakes.

9. To serve, bring the cheesecakes to room temperature, about 15 minutes. Garnish with the blueberry compote and white chocolate curls.

Mini Blueberry–White Chocolate Cheesecakes

Cookies and Confections

Pizzelle-Ferratelle

Italian Waffle Cookies

Pizzelle are traditional thin Italian waffle cookies originally made in the Abruzzo region. The name comes from the Italian word *pizze*, meaning round or flat. They are also known as *ferratelle, cancelle, neole,* or *osti*. *Pizzelle* are probably the most popular Italian wedding cookie, and I don't think I've ever seen an Italian cookie tray without one. Their shape and texture depend on the region the family is from. The story goes that a bride was never without a tray of *pizzelle* for her wedding guests. On the day of the wedding celebration, when the guests came to shower the bride and groom with gifts and admire the dowry, the bride would have a basket filled with *pizzelle* to offer her guests. The guests' acceptance of the *pizzelle* was a sign of well wishes and long happiness for the newly married couple. A very traditional filling is grape jam. *Pizzelle* can also be shaped into ice cream cones or edible ice cream cups. Enjoy with your favorite scoop of gelato.

To make these thin, crunchy cookies, you'll need a *pizzelle* maker, which is typically referred to as an iron because that is what they were originally made from. Today, the most popular *pizzelle* maker is electric. They are widely available at Italian grocers, kitchen stores, and online. When shaping the *pizzelle*, they must be hot and must be shaped immediately. They cool quickly and as they cool, they harden. *Pizzelle* can be stored in airtight containers or resealable plastic bags at room temperature for up to 1 week or in the freezer up to 3 months.

uno CREMA DI MASCARPONE (MASCARPONE CREAM)

½ cup (120 ml) cold heavy cream

7 tablespoons confectioners' sugar, sifted, divided

¾ cup (150 g) mascarpone cheese

grated zest of ½ lemon

½ teaspoon pure vanilla extract

due PIZZELLE (WAFFLE COOKIES)

6 large eggs, at room temperature

⅔ cup plus 2 tablespoons (180 ml) vegetable oil, divided

1⅓ cups (312 g) superfine sugar

3¾ cups (470 g) all-purpose flour

¾ teaspoon to 2 teaspoons anise seeds

1 teaspoon pure vanilla extract (optional)

finale ASSEMBLY

fresh berries, for garnish (for pizzelle cups)

sprinkles, chocolate chips, or nuts, for garnish (for rolled pizzelle)

uno TO MAKE THE MASCARPONE CREAM

1. In a small deep bowl, use a handheld mixer to beat the heavy cream at high speed until frothy.

2. Add 1 tablespoon confectioners' sugar and continue to beat at high speed until stiff peaks barely form.

3. In a second small deep bowl (you can use the same beaters; no need to wash them in between), beat the mascarpone at medium-high speed until creamy.

4. Add the remaining 6 tablespoons confectioners' sugar and the lemon zest and vanilla, and beat until smooth and creamy.

5. Using a medium flexible rubber spatula, fold half of the whipped cream into the mascarpone mixture. Fold in the remaining whipped cream until combined.

6. Refrigerate until ready to serve.

due TO MAKE THE WAFFLE COOKIES

1. Preheat a *pizzelle* iron according to the manufacturer's instructions. To prevent the cookies from sticking to the iron, it is best to let the hot iron sit for at least 10 minutes after it has come to baking temperature.

2. In a large bowl, use a handheld mixer to beat the eggs, ⅔ cup of the oil, and the sugar at medium-high speed until pale in color and fluffy, about 3 minutes.

3. Reduce the speed to medium-low. Gradually add the flour and beat until well combined.

4. Crush the anise seeds in a mortar and pestle, then add to the batter and beat to just combine. (Adjust the amount of anise seeds to suit your personal taste. I wouldn't add any more than 2 teaspoons for this amount of batter).

5. Add the vanilla, if using, and beat to just combine.

6. Place the remaining 2 tablespoons vegetable oil in a small bowl. Dip a spoon in the oil, tapping off any excess back into the bowl, and spoon a walnut-sized amount of dough onto the *pizzelle* iron. (Because the batter is so thick and sticky, dipping the spoon in oil makes getting the batter onto the iron much easier.) Bake until lightly golden, 45 to 60 seconds, depending on your iron. If you want a softer, chewier cookie, bake for less time and remove when very pale in color.

7. To serve the cookies plain and flat, transfer to a wire rack to cool. If you want a softer, chewier cookie, line the wire rack with a kitchen towel.

8. The cookies only stay soft for seconds, so to shape them into cups, working with one hot cookie at a time, center a cookie over a small cup, ramekin, or muffin cup and use a tart tamper to press the cookie gently into the cup. Hold securely for 1 minute while another *pizzelle* cooks on the iron. If you don't have a tart tamper, you can use two cups or ramekins of the same shape, one slightly

smaller than the other. Place the cookie in the large cup and fit the smaller cup inside it to create the shape. Hold securely for 1 minute.

9. To make rolled *pizzelle*, again working quickly with one hot cookie at a time, roll a cookie around a cannoli form. Hold securely for 1 minute while another *pizzelle* cooks on the iron, then remove the mold.

finale TO SERVE

1. To serve, transfer the mascarpone cream to a small pastry bag fitted with a large pastry tip of your choice. For waffle cups, pipe the cream into cups and garnish with fresh berries. For rolled *pizzelle*, insert the pastry tip into one side of the shell and gently squeeze until the shell is half full. Repeat on the other side. Garnish with sprinkles, chocolate chips, or nuts.

Italian Waffle Cookies

Soft Amaretti Cookies

Amaretti Morbidi

Soft Amaretti Cookies

Amaretti are my favorite cookies, period. To say I've struggled with making them is an understatement. After years of trying, I resorted to extreme measures—I kidnapped my mother and wouldn't allow her to leave until I perfected the technique. The trick for making the perfect tray of soft amaretti? Do not—and I repeat *do not*—overbeat the egg whites. Beat the egg whites to just shy of a soft peak and allow the cookie dough to rest in the fridge overnight before baking. For decorating, you'll find silver dragées available in kitchen supply stores with the cake decorating supplies, or online.

For these Amaretti cookies I've used store-bought almond meal, which is often labeled "almond flour." The almonds are blanched and the texture is quite fine but my mom always makes the cookies with homemade almond meal. It's not necessary to blanch the almonds if you are making homemade, but if you like the look of these cookies, blanched almonds are necessary.

3 large eggs

1⅓ cups (300 g) superfine sugar

4½ cups less ½ tablespoon (500 g) almond meal (made from blanched almonds), very finely ground

confectioners' sugar, sifted, for rolling

silver dragées, for decorating

1. Separate the eggs. Place the egg yolks in a large bowl and the egg whites in a second large bowl. Cover both bowls with plastic wrap, and allow to come to room temperature, about 30 minutes.

2. Using a large balloon whisk, beat the egg yolks, then gradually add the sugar while whisking until well combined.

3. Add the almond meal and whisk to just combine; do not overmix.

4. Using a clean, dry large balloon whisk, beat the egg whites to barely a soft peak. This is very, very important—do not overbeat.

5. Using a large flexible spatula, fold one-third of the egg whites into the almond mixture (this will loosen the almond mixture). Fold in the remaining egg whites just to combine; do not overmix.

6. Cover and refrigerate the cookie dough for at least 1 hour, or overnight for best results.

7. Preheat the oven to 325°F (160°C). Line 3 rimmed baking sheets with parchment paper or silicone baking mats.

8. Roll the cookie dough into ½-ounce balls. Roll the balls in confectioners' sugar and place a silver dragée in the center of each one. Do not flatten the cookies. Bake one sheet of cookies at a time, 20 cookies per sheet. Chill the remaining dough between batches.

9. Bake until barely light golden, 25 to 30 minutes, rotating the baking sheet halfway through.

10. Allow the cookies to cool on the baking sheet on a wire rack for two minutes. Using an offset spatula, transfer the cookies directly to the wire rack to cool completely.

Pasta Reale

MAKES ABOUT 48 (2½ TO 3½-INCH) MINI TARTS

Almond Tarts

I've used homemade almond meal made from blanched almonds, but store-bought almond meal, blanched or natural, can easily be substituted in this recipe. Occasionally I use store-bought almond meal, especially in recipes that call for a very fine grind. But usually I prefer to make the almond meal as needed. It's fresh, and in less than five minutes I can make almond meal at a fraction of the cost of store-bought products.

uno PASTRY DOUGH

6 large egg yolks

6 tablespoons (85 g) superfine sugar

2½ tablespoons (40 ml) vegetable oil

¼ teaspoon pure vanilla extract

2 cups (250 g) all-purpose flour

due ALMOND FILLING

1⅔ cups (250 g) blanched almonds (see page 20)

6 large egg whites

2⅔ cups (200 g) superfine sugar

finale ASSEMBLY

cooking spray, for coating the pans

confectioners' sugar, for dusting (optional)

uno TO MAKE THE PASTRY DOUGH

1. In a stand mixer fitted with the paddle attachment, beat the egg yolks, sugar, oil, and vanilla at medium speed until combined, 2 to 3 minutes.

2. Gradually add flour and beat to just combine.

3. Transfer the dough to a lightly floured work surface and knead until smooth, about 2 minutes. Shape into a ball, cover with plastic wrap, and let rest at room temperature for 30 minutes. While the dough rests, prepare the filling.

due TO MAKE THE ALMOND FILLING

1. In a food processor, process the blanched almonds until finely ground. Set aside.

2. In a stand mixer fitted with the whip attachment, beat the egg whites at medium speed until medium peaks form, about 8 minutes.

3. Gradually add the sugar, increase the speed to high, and beat for 1 minute.

4. Using a large flexible spatula, fold in the ground almonds.

finale TO ASSEMBLE

1. Preheat the oven to 350°F (180°C). Spray 2½ to 3½-inch mini tart pans with cooking spray.

2. Divide the dough into quarters. Work with one-quarter at a time, keeping the rest of the dough covered with plastic wrap to prevent it from drying out. Roll out the dough to ⅛ inch thick. Cut the dough into rounds large enough to cover the bottoms and sides of your tart pans. Use your fingers to fit the dough rounds into the pans. Using two small spoons, fill each tart shell with a dollop of almond filling to ⅛ inch from the top. Arrange the tarts on a rimmed baking sheet. Using a decorative pastry wheel, cut several strips of pastry dough about ¼ inch wide and place the strips on the tarts in a decorative crisscross pattern.

3. Bake until golden, 20 to 25 minutes.

4. Remove from the oven and immediately remove the tarts from the pans. If the dough sticks to the pans, use a toothpick or wooden skewer to help guide the tarts out. Transfer to a wire rack to cool. Repeat with the remaining dough and filling.

5. Dust with confectioners' sugar.

Almond Tarts

Bocconotti

Sweet Pastry Tartlets

Bocconotti, or *bocconotto*, originated in Castel Frentano, a small town in the province of Chieti in the Abruzzo region of Italy, a mere forty minutes from my family's hometown of Monteferrante. The traditional Abruzzi *bocconotti* are filled with toasted almonds and chocolate with a dusting of icing sugar. Pescara, a neighboring town, introduced a very strong Abruzzi liqueur, Centerba, which contains 70 percent alcohol, to the traditional filling. It is one of the strongest Italian liqueurs available. My father always kept a bottle tucked away in the china cabinet and it was only enjoyed when friends were visiting. I remember as a child being so fascinated by its striking green color and also the straw-covered bottle.

Today, the varying regions of Italy offer many different fillings in these tartlets, from jams and jellies to ricotta, custard, or nuts with fruit. *Bocconotti* should be made small enough to enjoy in one bite, but speaking from experience, one bite is never enough.

uno PASTRY DOUGH

7 tablespoons (100 g) vegetable shortening, melted and cooled

¼ cup plus 3 tablespoons (100 g) superfine sugar

3 large egg yolks

2¾ ounces (85 ml) dry vermouth

1 cup (125 g) all-purpose flour

¾ teaspoon baking powder

due CHOCOLATE-ALMOND FILLING

3 large egg whites

⅔ cup (150 g) superfine sugar

1 tablespoon (7 g) unsweetened cocoa, sifted

grated zest of ½ lemon

½ teaspoon pure vanilla extract

2¼ cups (300 g) almonds, toasted and finely chopped

½ cup (120 g) mini semisweet chocolate chips

finale ASSEMBLY

confectioners' sugar, for dusting

uno TO MAKE THE PASTRY DOUGH

1. In a stand mixer fitted with the paddle attachment, beat the shortening and sugar at medium speed for 2 minutes. Add the egg yolks and beat for 2 minutes longer. Add the vermouth and beat for 3 minutes longer.

2. Meanwhile, in a medium bowl, whisk together the flour and baking powder.

3. Gradually add the flour mixture to the shortening mixture and beat to just combine.

due TO MAKE THE CHOCOLATE-ALMOND FILLING

1. In a stand mixer fitted with the paddle attachment, beat the egg whites at medium speed until frothy. Add the sugar. Increase the speed to high and beat until the egg whites form stiff peaks.

2. Add the cocoa, lemon zest, and vanilla. Beat to just combine.

3. With a large rubber spatula, fold in the almonds and chocolate chips. Set aside.

finale TO ASSEMBLE

1. Preheat the oven to 350°F (180°C). Spray mini tart tins with ½-inch bases with cooking spray and set aside.

2. Scoop out 1 teaspoon of dough, roll it into a ball, and place it in a tart pan. Use your fingers to press the dough into the sides and bottom of the pan. Repeat with the remaining dough and tart pans. Arrange the pans on a full sheet pan.

3. Fill each tart shell with a large dollop of chocolate-almond filling. The tart should be almost overflowing because the filling tends to shrink, but make sure the filling does not touch the edge of the pastry where it meets the top of the pan because it could make the pastry stick.

4. Bake until golden, 20 to 25 minutes.

5. Remove the tins from the oven, and immediately remove the cookies from the tins (use a toothpick to help with removal if the pastry sticks). Transfer to a wire rack to cool completely. If baking in batches, wash and dry tins between uses.

6. To serve, dust with confectioner's sugar.

Sweet Pastry Tartlets

Celletti

Celletti

This is my family's classic *celletti* recipe. The name is the dialect translation for *uccelletti*, which means "birds" in Italian. *Mosto cotto*, made from concentrated reduced grape must (the grape juice extracted from the first press of a new wine), is a classic ingredient in Abruzzese cuisine and makes for a true, authentic-tasting *celletti*. It is quite sweet, and was a popular inexpensive substitute for sugar during World War II. My family makes our own *mosto cotto* during wine-making season, and it's a true labor of love, but you can also purchase it. *Celletti* are traditionally made with a combination of *mosto cotto* and marsala, but if *mosto cotto* is unavailable, increase the marsala in this recipe to ¾ cup and add ¼ cup sweet vermouth.

uno FILLING

¾ cup (180 ml) mosto cotto

¼ cup (60 ml) sweet marsala

½ tablespoon grated orange zest

1 teaspoon grated lemon zest

1 tablespoon plus 1 teaspoon (10 g) finely chopped walnuts

½ cup (50 g) plain finely ground bread crumbs

due PASTRY DOUGH

5 large eggs plus 1 large egg yolk

½ cup plus 1 tablespoon (130 ml) vegetable oil

½ cup plus 1 tablespoon (126 g) superfine sugar

1 package (9 g) vanilla sugar or 1 teaspoon pure vanilla extract

2 packages (32 g) lievito vaniglinato (yeast for cake with vanilla) (see page 8)

½ cup (120 ml) milk

4½ cups (563 g) all-purpose flour, divided

tre ICING

1 large egg white

1¼ cup plus 3 tablespoons (178 g) confectioners' sugar, sifted

1 teaspoon lemon juice

uno TO MAKE THE FILLING

1. In a small saucepan, heat the *mosto cotto*, marsala, orange zest, lemon zest, and walnuts over low heat until warmed through, and simmer for 2 minutes. Do not allow the mixture to boil.

2. Gradually add the bread crumbs. Cook, stirring constantly with a wooden spoon, until the mixture has the consistency of a soft jam, about 2 minutes.

3. Remove from the heat and set aside to cool.

due TO MAKE THE PASTRY DOUGH

1. Preheat the oven to 350°F (180°C). Line 3 rimmed baking sheets with parchment paper or silicone baking mats.

2. In a stand mixer fitted with the paddle attachment, beat the eggs, oil, sugar, and vanilla sugar or vanilla extract at medium speed for 4 minutes.

3. In a large cup, dissolve the *lievito vaniglinato* in the milk. Make sure to do this quickly because it will foam up. With the mixer running, immediately add the milk to the egg mixture, beating to combine.

4. Reduce the mixer speed to low and gradually add 3 cups (375 g) flour.

5. Remove the bowl from the mixer and fold in the remaining flour as best you can with a large flexible spatula.

6. Transfer the dough to a lightly floured work surface. Knead until smooth, 2 to 3 minutes. Shape into a ball. Cut the dough into quarters. Keep any unused dough covered with plastic wrap at all times to prevent it from drying out.

7. Working with one-quarter of dough at a time, roll each piece into a rectangle 4 to 4½ inches wide and ⅛ inch thick. It should resemble a sheet of pasta dough that has been run through a pasta machine.

8. Drop teaspoons of cooled filling about 4-inches apart on half the sheet of rolled dough, as if you were filling ravioli without a ravioli mold. Fold the other half of dough over the filling. Using a pastry wheel, cut each pillow into a half-moon shape. Join both ends together and place on a prepared baking sheet. Repeat until all the dough has been rolled and filled. If the dough trimmings are soft in texture, gather together and knead but refrain from adding flour (too much flour will dry out the pastry), reroll on a very lightly dusted with flour work surface and fill.

9. Bake until lightly golden, 15 to 20 minutes, rotating the baking sheets halfway through.

10. While the cookies are baking, prepare the icing.

tre TO MAKE THE ICING

1. In a small bowl, use a handheld mixer to beat the egg white at high speed until frothy.

2. Reduce the speed to low and gradually add the confectioners' sugar, then increase the speed to high and beat to stiff peaks.

3. Add the lemon juice and beat to just combine.

finale TO ASSEMBLE

1. When the cookies are finished baking, transfer the baking sheets to a wire rack. Working with one hot cookie at a time, use a clean kitchen towel to dust off the top. Use a small offset spatula (or your finger) to cover the top of the cookie with icing. (To keep your hands from burning, hold the cookie in the kitchen towel while icing). Transfer to a wire rack to cool. Repeat with the remaining cookies.

Pesche Dolci

Italian Peach Cookies

Pesche dolci, "sweet peaches," are festive Italian sandwich cookies generally reserved for special occasions. Feel free to substitute the peach jam for another flavor; the cookies are called "peaches" for their appearance, not necessarily their filling. The cream filling should be prepared when the cookie dough is resting, allowing plenty of time for chilling before assembling the cookies. Jam-filled cookies can be stored in an airtight container layered with parchment paper in the refrigerator for up to five days and in the freezer up to two months. Cream-filled cookies can be stored in an airtight container layered with parchment paper for up to 2 days. Keep in mind the cream-filled cookies are best enjoyed on the day they are made. If you prefer to make a full batch of small or large cookies, you will need to prepare extra filling.

uno COOKIES

3 large eggs, at room temperature

2 cups (450 g) superfine sugar

1 cup (240 ml) vegetable oil

3 tablespoons (18 g) vanilla sugar

2 tablespoons plus 2¾ teaspoons (21 g) lievito vaniglinato (*yeast for cake with vanilla*) (page 8)

1 cup (240 ml) whole milk

6 cups (750 g) all-purpose flour

due RIPIENI DI MARMELLATA DI PESCHE (PEACH JAM COOKIE FILLING)

cookie crumbs and bits from the baked cookies

2 cups (500 ml) peach jam

¼ ounce (½ tablespoon) rum, or to taste

finale ASSEMBLY

2 ounces dry vermouth

yellow liquid food coloring

red liquid food coloring

3 cups cold Crema Pasticcera (Pastry Cream) (page 10)

superfine sugar, for rolling cookies

1 vanilla bean, seeds removed (save seeds for another use), for decorating

fresh mint leaves, for decorating

uno TO MAKE THE COOKIES

1. In a stand mixer fitted with the paddle attachment, beat the sugar and eggs on medium speed until pale in color, 2 to 3 minutes.

2. Gradually add the oil, continuing to beat on medium speed. Add the vanilla sugar and beat to combine.

3. In a large cup, dissolve the baking powder in the milk, then add the milk to the batter. Continue to beat on medium speed until combined.

4. Reduce the mixer speed to low and gradually add the flour. Beat to just combine.

5. Let the batter stand at room temperature for 2 hours covered with a kitchen towel or plastic wrap before proceeding.

6. Preheat the oven to 350°F (180°) and position a rack in the middle of the oven. Line 2 rimmed baking sheets with parchment paper or silicone baking mats.

7. To form the cookies, wet your hands with a little bit of vegetable oil. For small cookies, roll about 1 teaspoon of dough into a ball; for large cookies, roll 2 teaspoons of dough. Be sure all the balls are the same size. Arrange 20 small balls of dough per baking sheet and 15 large balls of dough per baking sheet. Keep in mind you will need two cookies for each "peach."

8. Bake until the cookies just start to change color (you do not want them to turn golden), 15 to 17 minutes for small cookies, 20 to 25 minutes for large. Make sure to watch both small and large cookies at the 14-minute mark to determine baking time for your oven and the cookie size.

9. Immediately remove the cookies from the baking sheets and transfer to a wire rack.

10. Immediately begin hollowing out the cookies. Using a sharp paring knife and starting in the center of each cookie, carve small holes (about the size of a dime for small cookies and the size of a quarter for larger cookies), making sure you do not carve the holes too deep. Place the cookie bits and crumbs in a bowl and set aside. Return the hollowed cookies to the wire rack to cool completely prior to filling. Reserve the cookie crumbs.

11. When all cookies are baked and hollowed, take a few minutes to pair the cookies by size and set two aside for each "peach."

due TO MAKE THE PEACH JAM COOKIE FILLING

1. Place the reserved cookie crumbs and bits from the hollowed cookies in a food processor and pulse to a fine crumb.

2. In a small bowl, stir together the cookie crumbs and peach jam. If the jam is chunky, first purée it in a food processor until smooth.

3. Add the rum and stir to combine.

4. Cover and chill in the refrigerator until ready to fill the smaller cookies.

finale TO ASSEMBLE

1. Divide the dry vermouth between two small, deep bowls. Add yellow food coloring to one bowl and red food coloring to the other, enough to achieve a bright yellow and a bright red.

2. Transfer the pastry cream to a pastry bag fitted with a plain round tip. Place some superfine sugar on a flat plate for rolling the cookies, and set aside.

3. Pipe a small dollop of cream into the hollowed cavity of a large cookie. Join it with a second large cookie to form the "peach." Run your finger around the edge of each cookie to remove any excess filling. Repeat with the remaining large cookies.

4. Transfer the cold jam filling to a pastry bag fitted with a plain round tip. Pipe a small dollop of jam into the hollowed cavity of a small cookie. Join it with a second small cookie to form the "peach." Run your finger around the edge of each cookie to remove any excess filling. Repeat until all the small cookies are filled and formed.

5. To color the "peaches," working with one cookie at a time, stand a sandwiched cookie up so the filling line is perpendicular to your work surface. Dip the top half in yellow food coloring. Pat the cookie on a paper towel to remove any excess coloring, then dip the bottom half of the cookie in red food coloring, making sure it meets and overlaps the yellow half just a tad. Dab any excess coloring with a paper towel.

6. Roll the cookie in the sugar. Stand the cookie upright.

7. To decorate, cut the vanilla bean into thin strips resembling peach stems. Add a stem and a mint leaf to each cookie.

Italian Peach Cookies

Torrone di Mandorle Nocciole

MAKES 2 (8 X 11-INCH) BLOCKS AND 1 (4 X 11-INCH) BLOCK

Almond and Hazelnut Nougat

Torrone is a sweet nougat candy sandwiched between two sheets of very thin rice paper and often flavored with vanilla or citrus. Rice paper, also known as wafer paper, is actually made from potato starch, water, and vegetable oil, and comes in very thin sheets. I buy it by the sheet at my local bulk store, but you can find it in packages of 10 or 100 at baking supply stores and online. Instant-dissolving sugar, also called fruit sugar, is finely pulverized granulated sugar, but is not as fine as confectioners' sugar. The optimal condition for making the candy is when the temperature is cool and dry; heat and humidity can prevent the nougat from setting, leaving you with a sticky mess. *Torrone* keeps for a long time, making it the perfect choice for gift giving. Serve it with an after-dinner liqueur.

6 (8 x 11-inch) sheets rice (wafer) paper

3 large egg whites, at room temperature

2¼ cups (500 g) instant-dissolving sugar

1 (0.5-gram) package vanillina aroma per dolci (see page 8) or seeds of 1 vanilla bean or 2 teaspoons pure vanilla extract

2¼ cups (500 g) honey

3⅓ cups (500 g) toasted blanched almonds (about 1 pound) (see page 20)

6 cups (900 g) toasted skinned hazelnuts (about 2 pounds)

1. Arrange 3 rice paper sheets in a 1-inch-deep baking dish or a large rimmed baking sheet. Do not overlap the sheets.

2. In a stand mixer fitted with the whip attachment, beat the egg whites to soft peaks, starting on low speed and gradually increasing to high.

3. Decrease the mixer speed to low, and gradually add the sugar and then the *vanillina aroma* or the vanilla seeds or the vanilla extract. Increase the mixer speed to high and continue to beat the egg whites to stiff peaks.

4. Gradually add the honey and beat to combine well.

5. Transfer the honey–egg white mixture to a 6-quart nonstick pot. (A nonstick pot is essential because the mixture is very sticky.) Cook on low heat, stirring constantly with a wooden spoon or a large flexible spatula, until the mixture resembles melted marshmallows, 30 minutes.

6. Add the toasted almonds and hazelnuts and continue to cook on low heat, stirring constantly, until thickened, 30 minutes longer.

7. Remove from the heat. Spoon the mixture evenly over the rice paper, making sure to spread it all the way to the edges and corners of the pan. Cover with the remaining rice paper, making sure the top

108 GRACE'S SWEET LIFE

sheets line up with the bottom sheets, gently pressing down to level the nougat and to push out any air bubbles that may have formed. Set aside to cool.

8. Turn out the nougat onto a cutting board. To easily cut into pieces, place a serrated knife blade on the nougat and push down on blade with your palms, then use a sawing motion to cut through the bottom layer of rice paper. Cut into squares, rectangles, or triangles.

9. Store in an airtight container in a cool, dry place for 3 to 4 weeks.

Almond and Hazelnut Nougat

Salame al Cioccolato

Chocolate Salami

This extra-special Italian treat is traditionally made with three main ingredients: chocolate, cookies, and dark rum. You can simply slice it on a platter, or to serve the salami in true Italian style, place the log on a wooden board along with a knife and allow your guests to cut their own slices. Serve with after-dinner liqueurs, freshly brewed espresso or coffee, and of course, fresh fruit. The chocolate salami will be firm when you first remove it from the refrigerator. It is best to cut slices immediately but then allow it to come to room temperature before serving. Note that this recipe uses raw eggs; please make sure to use only the freshest. *Salame al cioccolato* can be stored well wrapped in the refrigerator for up to one week or well wrapped and sealed in an airtight container in the freezer for up to one month.

8 ounces (226 g) good-quality dark chocolate, 70%, finely chopped

¼ cup plus 3 tablespoons (100 g) unsalted butter, at room temperature

⅔ cup (150 g) superfine sugar

3 large eggs, lightly beaten

2 tablespoons (30 ml) dark rum

½ teaspoon pure vanilla extract

2 tablespoons (15 g) unsweetened cocoa, sifted

about 9 ounces (250 g) plain cookies (like tea biscuits or digestive cookies), coarsely chopped

½ cup (75 g) toasted almonds, finely chopped (see page 20)

½ cup (75 g) toasted skinned hazelnuts, finely chopped (see page 20)

⅓ cup (50 g) toasted unsalted shelled pistachios, finely chopped (see page 20)

confectioners' sugar, sifted, as needed

1. Place the chocolate in a heatproof bowl set over a saucepan of just-simmering water (do not let the bowl touch the water). Stir until the chocolate is melted and smooth. Remove from the heat and set aside to cool.

2. In a medium bowl, whisk the butter and sugar until creamy. Add the eggs and whisk until well combined. Add the rum and vanilla, and whisk to combine.

3. Add the cocoa to cooled melted chocolate and stir until well combined.

4. Add the chocolate mixture to the egg mixture and whisk until well combined.

5. Add the cookies, almonds, hazelnuts, and pistachios to the mixture. Stir with a wooden spoon to combine well.

6. Cover and refrigerate the mixture until firm, about 30 minutes.

7. Using a fine-mesh sieve, sift confectioners' sugar over a clean work surface. Transfer the chocolate-cookie mixture to the work surface on top of the sugar.

8. Using your hands, form the chocolate-cookie mixture into a log like a salami about 2 inches in diameter.

9. Using the fine-mesh sieve, sift more confectioners' sugar over the surface of the log to coat well.

10. Place the log on a sheet of plastic wrap and wrap tightly. Grasp both ends of the plastic wrap and twist by rolling the log toward you several times. Wrap as tightly as possible to keep the log shape. To secure, tie a knot at each end. To make the chocolate salami look authentic, tie kitchen string around the log to resemble sausage netting.

11. Refrigerate for at least 3 hours, preferably overnight.

12. To serve, slice the cold salami and allow the slices to come to room temperature.

Chocolate Salami

Pies and Tarts

Crostata di Fragole con Crema Diplomatica

Strawberry Tart with Lightened Pastry Cream

This summer tart is filled with *crema diplomatica*, a combination of my two favorite creams: *crema pasticcera* and *crema chantilly*. Also called *crème chiboust*, it is light, flavorful, and delicious, and the perfect pillow for fresh seasonal berries. Traditionally, the combination is two parts pastry cream to one part chantilly cream, but in this recipe I've used almost equal amounts of both because I wanted a lighter, airier version, and I also wanted the pure vanilla flavor to shine through.

uno TART SHELL

   Pasta Frolla alle Nocciole (Hazelnut Sweet Pastry Dough) (page 18)

due CREMA DIPLOMATICA

   2¼ cups (125 g) cold Crema Chantilly (Chantilly Cream) (page 12)

   3 cups (250 g) Crema Pasticcera (Pastry Cream) (page 10)

tre GLASSA ALLA MARMELLATA CON GRAND MARNIER (GRAND MARNIER–APRICOT GLAZE)

   ½ cup (120 ml) pure apricot jam

   1 tablespoon (15 ml) orange marmalade

   2 tablespoons (30 ml) water

   1 tablespoon (15 ml) Grand Marnier

finale ASSEMBLY

   2 to 3 cups (450 to 700 g) fresh strawberries, hulled and sliced

uno TO MAKE THE TART SHELL

1. Lightly knead the pastry dough, and divide the dough into two portions; two-thirds is needed for this tart. Shape each portion into a ball, and pat the larger portion into a disk. Cover the smaller ball with a kitchen towel to keep it from drying out.

2. Roll out the disk of dough into a 14-inch circle about ⅛ inch thick. Fit the dough into an 11-inch tart pan and trim any excess with a sharp paring knife. Pierce the bottom of the pastry shell with a fork.

3. Transfer the pastry shell dish to a rimmed baking sheet. Cover with plastic wrap and freeze until firm, about 30 minutes, to help prevent the pastry from shrinking when it is baked.

4. Add any excess dough to the remaining one-third of the dough. Quickly re-roll and shape it into a ball, pat it into a disk, and cover with plastic wrap. Refrigerate for up to 1 week or store the plastic-wrapped pastry in a resealable bag or an airtight container in the freezer for up to 1 month.

5. Preheat the oven to 375°F (190°C).

6. Remove the pastry shell from the freezer. To blind-bake the pastry to prevent it from shrinking, line the shell with parchment paper and fill with ceramic pie weights, or uncooked rice or beans, flush to the top. Bake for 20 minutes. Transfer the tart pan to a wire rack, remove the weights and parchment paper, and then return to the oven to bake until lightly golden, 5 to 10 minutes.

7. Transfer the pastry shell to a wire rack to cool in the baking pan until warm to the touch and then remove from the pan and return to the wire rack to cool completely.

due TO MAKE THE CREMA DIPLOMATICA

1. Using a large flexible spatula, fold one-third of the cold chantilly cream into the pastry cream to lighten, then fold in the remaining chantilly cream.

2. Transfer to an airtight container and refrigerate until ready to use.

tre TO MAKE THE GRAND MARNIER–APRICOT GLAZE

1. In a small saucepan over medium heat, combine the jam, marmalade, and water and stir until melted.

2. Strain the mixture through a fine-mesh sieve into a small heatproof bowl, making sure to scrape the pulp on the underside of the sieve (discard any solids).

3. Stir in the Grand Marnier.

finale TO ASSEMBLE

1. If needed, reheat the Grand Marnier–apricot glaze over low heat.

2. Place the cool pastry shell on serving dish or cake stand. Using a large pastry brush, coat the base of the pastry shell with a thin layer of warm apricot glaze. Set aside to set for 15 minutes.

3. Fill the pastry shell with *crema diplomatica*. Use an offset spatula to spread the cream evenly to the edges.

4. Decoratively arrange the strawberry slices on top of the cream, then use a pastry brush to lightly coat the strawberries with apricot glaze.

5. If not serving immediately, cover and refrigerate the tart. Remove it from the refrigerator 20 to 30 minutes before serving to come to room temperature.

Strawberry Tart with Lightened Pastry Cream

Tartellette alla Crema di Limone e Meringa all'Italiana

Lemon Meringue Tartlets

uno TART SHELLS

Pasta Frolla 1 (Sweet Pastry Dough) (page 17)

due CREMA DI LIMONE (LEMON CREAM)

¼ cup plus 1 teaspoon (65 ml) heavy cream

½ cup (120 ml) freshly squeezed lemon juice (from about 2 lemons)

grated zest of 1 lemon

4 large egg yolks, at room temperature

½ cup (113 g) superfine sugar

¼ cup plus 1 tablespoon (70 g) unsalted butter, at room temperature, cut into 10 equal pieces

finale ASSEMBLY

1 large egg, lightly beaten, for egg wash

Meringa all'Italiana (Italian Meringue) (page 15)

uno TO MAKE THE TART SHELLS

1. Lightly knead the pastry dough, and divide the dough in half. Shape each half into a ball and pat each ball down into a disk. One disk of dough is required for the tarts. Store the second disk of dough according to recipe instructions.

2. Roll out the remaining dough to ⅛ inch thick.

3. Working quickly, cut the dough into 6 (6-inch) rounds. Fit the rounds into 4½-inch tart pans and trim any excess dough with a sharp knife. Pierce the bottoms of the pastry shells with a fork.

4. Transfer the tart pans to a rimmed baking sheet and freeze until firm, about 30 minutes, to help prevent the pastry from shrinking when it is baked.

5. Preheat the oven to 325°F (160°C).

6. Remove the pastry shells from the freezer. To blind bake the pastry to prevent it from shrinking, line the shells with parchment paper, leaving a 1-inch overhang, then fill with ceramic pie weights, or dried beans or rice, flush to the top. Bake until the edges just begin to turn golden, 20 to 25 minutes.

due TO MAKE THE LEMON CREAM

1. In a small saucepan over medium heat, bring the heavy cream and lemon juice and zest to a boil.

2. In a medium bowl, whisk the egg yolks and sugar until pale in color.

3. In a slow, steady stream, gradually pour the hot cream mixture into the egg mixture, whisking constantly until well combined.

4. Pour the egg-cream mixture into the saucepan and bring to a boil over medium heat, whisking constantly.

5. Continue to cook, whisking constantly, until the mixture thickens, about 5 minutes.

6. Strain the lemon cream through a fine-mesh sieve into a medium heatproof bowl. Whisk in the butter two pieces at a time.

7. Place a sheet of plastic wrap directly on the surface of the lemon cream to prevent a skin from forming while it cools. Refrigerate for at least 30 minutes before filling the tarts.

finale TO ASSEMBLE

1. Remove the pastry shells from the oven and transfer the baking sheet to a wire rack. Remove the parchment paper and pie weights. Let the shells cool for 2 minutes.

2. Brush the lightly beaten egg on the base of each pastry shell. Bake until golden all over, 5 to 10 minutes.

3. Transfer the baking sheet to a wire rack and cool for 2 to 3 minutes. Remove the shells from the pans and transfer directly to the wire rack to cool completely.

4. While the pastry shells cool, prepare the Italian meringue.

5. Transfer the cold lemon cream to a large pastry bag fitted with a large plain tip. Pipe the lemon cream into the cooled pastry shells. If you don't have a pastry bag, spoon the cream into the shells.

6. Transfer the meringue to a large pastry bag fitted with a large plain tip. Pipe the meringue in peaks on top of the lemon cream. You can also spoon meringue onto the lemon cream and use the back of a spoon to create peaks.

7. To brown the tips and sides of peaks, run a crème brûlée torch back and forth across the top of the meringue. Don't hold the torch in one place for too long because the meringue easily scorches. If you do not have a torch, preheat the oven's broiler. Arrange the tarts on a rimmed baking sheet and place them under the broiler. Watch the tarts very carefully, as the meringue can brown quite quickly. It is best to turn the baking sheet a few times to ensure even browning.

8. Transfer the tarts to a wire rack to cool. Remove from the baking sheet and serve.

9. Tarts can be stored in an airtight container in the refrigerator.

Crostata al Cioccolato con Glassa al Cioccolato

Chocolate Truffle Tart with Chocolate Glaze

To make this tart, you'll need an 8½ x 1-inch round tart pan with a removable bottom.

uno CROSTA DI BISCOTTI AL CIOCCOLATO (CHOCOLATE COOKIE CRUST)

1½ cups (136 g) chocolate cookie crumbs or 23 chocolate wafer cookies (about 5 ounces or 140 g), finely ground

5 tablespoons (71 g) unsalted butter, melted

due RIPIENO DI CREMA AL CIOCCOLATO (CHOCOLATE TRUFFLE FILLING)

8¾ ounces (250 g) good-quality bittersweet chocolate, 60%, finely chopped

¼ cup plus 2 tablespoons (85 g) unsalted butter, cut into 6 pieces, at room temperature

2 large eggs, lightly beaten

⅓ cup (80 ml) heavy cream

⅓ cup to ⅓ cup plus 2 tablespoons (75 to 103 g) superfine sugar, or as needed

¼ teaspoon salt

1 teaspoon pure vanilla extract

tre GLASSA AL CIOCCOLATO (CHOCOLATE GLAZE)

2¼ ounces (64 g) good-quality bittersweet chocolate, 60%, or semisweet chocolate, finely chopped

2½ tablespoons heavy cream

1¼ teaspoons dark corn syrup

1¼ tablespoons warm water

quattro CREMA DI MASCARPONE (MASCARPONE CREAM)

¾ cup (180 ml) cold heavy cream

1½ tablespoons confectioners' sugar, sifted

1 teaspoon vanilla extract

¾ cup plus 1 tablespoon (163 g) mascarpone cheese, at room temperature

uno TO MAKE THE CHOCOLATE COOKIE CRUST

1. Preheat the oven to 350°F (180°C).

2. In a small bowl, stir together the cookie crumbs and melted butter until combined and evenly moistened.

3. Press the crumb mixture evenly into the base and up the sides of the tart pan.

4. Place the crumb-lined pan on a sheet of aluminum foil (in case the butter leaks) and bake until slightly puffed, about 10 minutes.

5. Transfer to a wire rack to cool for 10 minutes.

due TO MAKE THE CHOCOLATE TRUFFLE FILLING

1. Melt the chocolate and butter in a heatproof bowl set over a pan of just-simmering water, stirring occasionally (do not let the bowl touch the water). Set aside and allow to cool slightly, about 5 minutes.

2. In a medium bowl, whisk together the eggs, cream, ⅓ cup sugar, salt, and vanilla.

3. Add the cooled chocolate mixture and whisk to combine. Taste, and if you would prefer it sweeter, add the remaining 2 tablespoons sugar a little at a time as needed.

4. Pour the filling through a fine-mesh sieve into the cooled tart shell. (You may need a helper to hold the sieve, and remember to scrape the chocolate from the underside of the sieve). Tap the tart pan once on countertop to remove any air bubbles. (If any air bubbles are visible after tapping, use the tip of a sharp paring knife or toothpick to pop them; this will make for better presentation).

5. Bake in the 350°F (180°C) oven until the filling is slightly puffed, set around edges, and the center jiggles slightly when the pan is gently shaken (the filling will continue to set as the tart cools), 20 to 25 minutes.

6. Transfer to a wire rack and cool completely in the pan, about 1 hour.

7. When the tart is cool, prepare the chocolate glaze.

tre TO MAKE THE CHOCOLATE GLAZE

1. Place the chocolate in small heatproof bowl.

2. In small saucepan, bring the cream to a boil over medium-low heat.

3. Immediately pour the hot cream over the chocolate and let stand for 1 minute.

4. Using a small, flexible spatula, stir the chocolate and cream together. Begin near the center of the bowl and gradually work your way toward the edges, pulling in as much chocolate as possible, until the glaze is smooth, glossy, and well combined.

5. Stir in the corn syrup, then the warm water.

6. Strain the glaze through a fine-mesh sieve into a 1-cup liquid measuring cup. (Remember to scrape the underside of the sieve.)

7. Immediately pour the glaze into the center of the cooled tart. Working quickly, use an offset spatula to spread the glaze evenly to the edges leaving a ¼ inch border.

8. Let stand until the glaze is set, about 1 hour.

quattro TO MAKE THE MASCARPONE CREAM

1. In a medium bowl and using a handheld mixer, beat the cream, confectioners' sugar, and vanilla at high speed until soft peaks form.

2. In a second medium bowl, use a handheld mixer to beat the mascarpone cheese at medium speed until smooth and creamy.

3. Using a large flexible spatula, gently fold the cream mixture into mascarpone.

4. Transfer the mascarpone cream to an airtight container, cover, and refrigerate for 30 minutes.

finale TO SERVE

1. Form the cold mascarpone cream into quenelles: Dip two spoons in hot water and dry with a clean kitchen towel. Scoop a generous portion of the mixture with one spoon. With the second spoon, carefully press the spoon on the mixture and roll the spoon to the right, twisting your wrist up to scoop up the mixture. This forces the food into an oval shape. Using this method, transfer the quenelle from one spoon to the other several times to create a smooth, even shape.

2. To serve the tart, garnish each slice with a quenelle of mascarpone cream.

Chocolate Truffle Tart with Chocolate Glaze

Tartellette al Cioccolato e Caramello con Nocciole

Chocolate, Caramel, and Hazelnut Tartlets

If there were ever a dessert you wish you'd made more of, this would be it. The first time I made these tarts I was hosting an outdoor barbecue and I decided to prepare a tasting table of sweet treats. I remember walking in and out of the house bringing out trays of different treats, but when I walked out with the tarts all eyes were suddenly on the tarts and instantly I wished I'd made more. This recipe only requires half of the *pasta frolla* recipe, but you might seriously want to think about doubling the recipe because these disappear quickly. If you can't find liquid glucose, increase the superfine sugar in the caramel to 1⅓ cup plus 1½ tablespoons.

uno TART SHELLS

½ recipe Pasta Frolla alle Nocciole (Hazelnut Sweet Pastry Dough)

1 large egg, lightly beaten, for egg wash

due CARAMELLO (CARAMEL)

1 cup plus 1 teaspoon (230 g) superfine sugar

⅓ cup plus 1 tablespoon (90 ml) liquid glucose

¾ cup plus 2 tablespoons (210 ml) heavy cream, at room temperature

3 tablespoons (43 g) unsalted butter

tre GANACHE DI CIOCCOLATO (CHOCOLATE GANACHE)

2¾ ounces (78 g) good-quality dark chocolate (70%), finely chopped

1½ ounces (43 g) good-quality milk chocolate, finely chopped

½ cup plus 1½ teaspoons (125 ml) heavy cream

1½ tablespoons (21 g) unsalted butter, at room temperature

¼ cup (40 g) toasted, skinned, and halved hazelnuts (see page 20)

quattro GLASSA AL CIOCCOLATO DI LATTE (MILK CHOCOLATE GLAZE)

½ cup (120 ml) heavy cream

4 ounces (113 g) good-quality milk chocolate, finely chopped

finale ASSEMBLY

Panna Montata Zuccherata (Sweetened Whipped Cream) (optional) (page 13)

Pralina di Nocciole (Hazelnut Praline) (optional) (page 21)

uno TO MAKE THE TART SHELLS

1. Lightly knead the hazelnut sweet pastry dough, and divide the dough in half. Shape each half into a ball and pat each ball down into a disk. One disk of dough is required for the tarts. Store the remaining dough in the freezer according to recipe instructions.

2. Working quickly, roll out dough to ⅛ inch thick. Cut the dough into 6 (6-inch) rounds. Fit the rounds into 4½-inch tart pans and trim any excess pastry with a sharp paring knife. Pierce the bottoms of the pastry shells with a fork.

3. Transfer the tins to a rimmed baking sheet and chill the pastry shells in the freezer for 30 minutes to prevent the pastry from shrinking while it bakes.

4. Preheat the oven to 325°F (160°C).

5. Remove the pastry shells from freezer. To blind bake the pastry to prevent it from shrinking, line the shells with parchment paper, leaving a 1-inch overhang, and fill with ceramic pie weights, or uncooked rice or beans, flush to the top. Bake until lightly golden around the edges, 20 to 25 minutes.

6. Transfer the baking sheet to a wire rack. Remove the parchment paper and pie weights. Cool for 2 minutes, and then brush the bottoms of the pastry shells with the egg wash. Return to the oven and bake until golden all over, 5 to 10 minutes.

7. Transfer the pastry shells in the pans to a wire rack and cool for 3 to 4 minutes. Remove from the pans and return to the wire rack to cool completely.

8. While the tarts are cooling, prepare the caramel.

due TO MAKE THE CARAMEL

1. In a medium saucepan over low heat, stir together the sugar and glucose until the sugar dissolves and the syrup comes to a boil.

2. Increase the heat to medium and cook the syrup, occasionally swirling the pan over the burner (do not stir), until it reaches a light-brown color, about 5 minutes. Use a pastry brush dipped in water to wash down any crystals that form on the sides of the pan.

3. Carefully and gradually add the heavy cream (the caramel will splatter and boil up), whisking constantly until smooth. There should be no lumps of hardened sugar; if any remain, return the pan to the heat and whisk until smooth.

4. Remove from the heat and allow the caramel to cool slightly, about 3 minutes.

5. Whisk in the butter until smooth and glossy. Using a fine-mesh sieve, strain the caramel into a small bowl (discard any solids). Straining the caramel is optional, but it will ensure a smooth sauce by catching any bits of hardened sugar that didn't melt.

6. Fill the cooled pastry shells just a bit more than one-third full with caramel. Refrigerate until set, about 20 minutes.

7. While the tarts refrigerate, prepare the chocolate ganache.

tre TO MAKE THE CHOCOLATE GANACHE

1. Place the dark chocolate and milk chocolate in a small heatproof bowl.

2. In a small saucepan, bring the cream just to a boil over medium heat.

3. Remove from the heat. Pour cream over chocolate, making sure the chocolate is completely covered. Let stand for 2 minutes.

4. Stir with a flexible rubber spatula until smooth. Add the butter and stir until well combined.

5. Remove the tarts from the refrigerator and arrange a layer of the toasted, halved hazelnuts on top of the caramel.

6. Spoon the ganache over the hazelnuts, filling to a little more than one-third from the top of the pastry shell.

7. Return the tarts to the refrigerator until set, about 30 minutes. While the tarts refrigerate, prepare the chocolate glaze.

quattro TO MAKE THE MILK CHOCOLATE GLAZE

1. In a small saucepan over medium heat, bring the cream just to a boil.

2. Remove from the heat. Add the chocolate, making sure the cream completely covers it. Let stand for 2 minutes.

3. Stir with a flexible rubber spatula until smooth. Strain the glaze through a fine-mesh sieve into a small bowl (discard any solids).

4. Remove the tarts from the refrigerator. Spoon the chocolate glaze to the top of each pastry shell.

5. Return the tarts to the refrigerator until set, 20 to 30 minutes or until ready to serve.

finale TO ASSEMBLE AND SERVE

1. When ready to serve, remove the tarts from the refrigerator and allow to come to room temperature.

2. Reheat the caramel until smooth.

3. Transfer the whipped cream to a large pastry bag fitted with a decorative tip (I like a Wilton 1M). Pipe a swirl of whipped cream in the center of each tart.

4. Transfer the caramel to a squeeze bottle and drizzle over the tarts. (If you don't have a squeeze bottle, drizzle the caramel with a spoon.)

5. If using hazelnut praline, place a few pieces at a time in a food processor, pulsing until you reach a coarse crumb. For these tarts, you want a crunchy texture to contrast the smooth creamy filling. If you prefer, place pieces of praline in a plastic bag, seal, and use a rolling pin or mallet to crush into smaller pieces. Sprinkle the praline over the tarts.

Pasticciotti Leccesi

MAKES 6 TO 8 MEDIUM (2¾ X 1½-INCH) TARTS

Custard Tarts

Pasticciotti are generally served for breakfast, but of course they can be enjoyed at any time of the day. Traditionally, the oval-shaped pastries are filled with pastry cream and made with plain sweet pastry dough. I've prepared these pastries using *pasta frolla al cacao* (chocolate sweet pastry dough, page 18), but you can make it with plain *pasta frolla* (page 17) if you prefer to enjoy the traditional; for plain pastry dough, add 1 tablespoon milk to the egg wash, and dust the tarts with confectioners' sugar when they're hot from the oven. Today, custard tarts are served not only with pastry cream but also with a layer of jam, Nutella, or *crema pasticcera al cioccolato* (chocolate pastry cream) and one of my favorites, *crema pasticcera al mandorle* (almond pastry cream).

uno TART SHELLS

Pasta Frolla al Cacao (Chocolate Sweet Pastry Dough) (page 18)

due FILLING

3 cups Crema Pasticcera (Pastry Cream) (page 10)

finale ASSEMBLY

1 large egg white, lightly beaten

sanding (decorating) sugar

uno TO MAKE THE TART SHELLS

1. Divide the chocolate pastry dough in two, and make one piece slightly larger than the other (the larger piece will be used to line the pastry tins, and the smaller piece will be used to top the tarts). Shape each piece into a ball. Flatten each ball into a disc, and wrap tightly in plastic. Refrigerate the discs for at least 1 hour prior to rolling.

due TO MAKE THE FILLING

1. Meanwhile, while the dough is chilling, strain the pastry cream into a 9 x 13-inch baking dish (discard the solids) and place a sheet of plastic wrap directly on the surface of the cream to prevent a skin from forming as it cools. Allow to cool completely.

finale TO ASSEMBLE

1. Transfer the larger piece of chilled pastry dough to a lightly floured work surface (keep the smaller piece refrigerated). Working quickly, roll out the dough to about ¼ inch (6 mm) thick.

2. Cut each pastry round slightly larger than your tart pans. Line the base and sides of each pan with a pastry round, leaving a slight overhang.

3. Fill each pan almost to the top with pastry cream. Set aside.

126 GRACE'S SWEET LIFE

4. Remove the remaining pastry dough from the refrigerator. Roll out the dough to about ¼-inch (6 mm) thick. Cut the dough into rounds large enough to cover each pan.

5. Place the pastry rounds over the tarts and pinch the edges to seal. Reroll any pastry scraps, cut additional rounds (two per tin), fill and cover. Use a small pastry brush to brush the tops of the tarts with the egg white, and sprinkle the sanding sugar on top.

6. Arrange the pans on a rimmed baking sheet and refrigerate for 30 minutes.

7. Preheat the oven to 350°F (180°C). Bake the tarts for 15 minutes, then increase the oven temperature to 390°F (200°C) and continue to bake until the top crust is dry, about 10 minutes longer (because the pastry is so dark to begin with, it's best to watch the tarts in the last 5 to 7 minutes of baking time; if necessary cover with aluminum foil to prevent the tops from burning before the pastry is cooked).

8. Transfer the tarts to a wire rack to cool slightly. Carefully remove tarts from the pans. *Pasticciotti* are best enjoyed warm.

Custard Tarts

Crostata di Mele con Calvados

Apple Pie with Calvados

uno CRUST

> *Pasta Brisè per Crostate (Pie Dough) (page 20)*

due RIPIENO DI MELE CON CALVADOS (APPLE PIE FILLING WITH CALVADOS)

> *1⅓ to 1⅔ pounds (604 to 755 grams) Honey Crisp and Granny Smith apples, peeled, cored, and cut into ⅛-inch-thick slices (about 4 to 5 medium apples)*
>
> *juice of 1 lemon*
>
> *⅔ cup (150 ml) whole milk*
>
> *⅔ cup (150 ml) heavy cream*
>
> *¼ cup (60 ml) calvados (apple brandy)*
>
> *¼ cup plus 2 tablespoons (85 grams) superfine sugar*
>
> *seeds of 1 vanilla bean*
>
> *2 large eggs plus 1 large egg yolk*
>
> *pinch of salt*

finale ASSEMBLY

> *2 tablespoons (26 grams) light brown sugar, for sprinkling (optional)*
>
> *¼ cup (60 ml) apricot jam*
>
> *1 tablespoon water*

uno TO MAKE THE CRUST

1. Divide the pie dough into 2 balls, using about two-thirds of the dough for one ball and the remaining dough for the second ball. Flatten each ball into a disk, wrap in plastic, and refrigerate for 1 hour.

2. Remove the larger disc of dough from the refrigerator. Reserve the remaining disk of dough for another use. (Leftover dough can be stored, well wrapped, in the freezer for up to 1 month.) Transfer the pastry to a clean, lightly floured work surface and roll out to a 14-inch circle, about ⅛ inch thick. Dust off the excess flour with a pastry brush. (If the pastry dough becomes soft or sticky, return to the refrigerator to firm up.) Lightly flour the rolling pin, and roll the circle of dough up onto the rolling pin and carefully transfer to an 11-inch tart pan. Fit the dough into the tart pan; trim off any excess pastry with a sharp paring knife. Pierce the bottom of the pastry shell with a fork. Chill in the freezer until firm, about 30 minutes.

3. Preheat the oven to 350°F (180°C). Remove the pastry shell from the freezer. To blind bake the pastry to prevent it from shrinking, line the shell with parchment paper, leaving a 2-inch overhang, and fill with ceramic pie weights, or uncooked rice or beans, flush to the top. Bake for 15 minutes. Transfer the tart pan to a wire rack; carefully remove the weights and parchment paper, and then return to the oven to bake until lightly golden, about 10 minutes.

due TO MAKE THE APPLE PIE FILLING WITH CALVADOS

1. Place the apple slices in a medium bowl. To prevent the apples from browning, pour the lemon juice over the slices and toss to coat.

2. To make the custard, in a large pourable container, whisk together the milk, cream, calvados, sugar, vanilla seeds, eggs, egg yolk, and salt until the sugar is dissolved and mixture is well combined.

finale TO ASSEMBLE

1. Remove the pastry shell from the oven and transfer to a wire rack. Increase the oven temperature to 375°F (190°C).

2. Arrange the apple slices in the pastry shell, overlapping them in a radial design (the apple slices will shrink while baking; arranging more apple slices is better than using too few). Make a second circle of slices; arranging the slices in the opposite direction. Repeat with a third circle if necessary, arranging the slices in the opposite direction.

3. Carefully pour the filling evenly over the apples. Sprinkle with brown sugar, if using.

4. Return to the preheated oven and bake until the pastry is golden and the custard is almost set but still moist (it should jiggle slightly when tart pan is gently shaken), about 40 minutes.

5. Just before the crostata is ready to remove from the oven, prepare the apricot glaze. In a small saucepan over medium heat, combine the apricot jam and water, stirring until the mixture becomes a liquid. Remove from the heat and strain through a fine-mesh sieve into a small bowl.

6. Remove the crostata from the oven and transfer to a wire rack. Using a large pastry brush, coat the apple slices with warm apricot glaze. Serve warm.

Apple Pie with Calvados

Tartellette con Crema Pasticcera e Frutti di Bosco

MAKES 8 (4½-INCH) TARTS

Tartlets with Pastry Cream and Mixed Berries

These tarts use only about two-thirds of the *pasta frolla* recipe. I usually roll out the remaining dough, bake it in tart pans, and then store the baked shells in the freezer for another use. They're convenient to have on hand for last-minute desserts. To make these tarts, you'll need eight 4½-inch tart pans with removable bottoms.

uno TART SHELLS

Pasta Frolla 1 (Sweet Pastry Dough) (page 17)

1 large egg, lightly beaten, for egg wash

finale ASSEMBLY

1½ cups (125 g) Crema Pasticcera (Pastry Cream) (page 10)

½ cup plus ½ tablespoon (125 ml) cold heavy cream

½ tablespoon confectioners' sugar, sifted

¼ cup (60 ml) cherry jelly, seedless raspberry jam, apricot jam, or red currant jelly

raspberries, blueberries, and blackberries

uno TO MAKE THE TART SHELLS

1. Lightly knead the pastry dough, and divide the dough in two, making one piece about two-thirds of the dough and the second piece the remaining third. Shape each piece into a ball and pat each ball into a disk. Wrap each disk in plastic wrap. Refrigerate larger disk for 1 hour. Store the remaining dough in the freezer according to the recipe instructions.

2. Roll out the dough on a lightly floured work surface to ⅛ inch thick. Cut the pastry into 8 (6-inch) rounds. Fit the pastry rounds into 8 (4½-inch) tart pans, and trim any excess pastry with a sharp paring knife. Pierce the base of each pastry shell with a fork. Arrange the tins on a baking sheet cover and freeze until firm, about 30 minutes, to prevent the pastry from shrinking when baked.

3. Preheat the oven to 375°F (190°C).

4. Remove the pastry shells from the freezer. Line each pastry shell with parchment paper, leaving a 1-inch overhang, and fill with ceramic pie weights, or uncooked beans or rice. Bake until edges just begin to turn golden, about 15 minutes.

5. Transfer the baking sheet to a wire rack. Remove the parchment paper and pie weights. Let cool for 2 minutes. Lightly brush the base of each pastry shell with the egg wash. Return to the oven and continue to bake until golden all over, 5 to 10 minutes.

6. Transfer the pastry shells to a wire rack and allow to cool in the pans, 2 to 3 minutes. Remove the pastry shells from the pans and return to the wire rack to cool completely.

finale TO ASSEMBLE

1. In a small saucepan, heat the jelly or jam over medium-low heat, stirring constantly, until melted. Using a fine-mesh sieve, strain the jam or jelly into a small bowl, making sure to scrape the jelly on the underside of the sieve (discard the solids). Set aside to cool slightly.

2. In small bowl, use a handheld mixer to beat the heavy cream and confectioners' sugar to soft peaks. Gently fold one-half of the whipped cream into the pastry cream (this will help loosen the mixture), then fold in remaining whipped cream. Divide the pastry cream evenly among the pastry shells. Using a small offset spatula, spread the cream evenly to the edges of the shells.

3. Decoratively arrange the berries on top of each tart. Using a small pastry brush, thinly coat the berries with the melted jam glaze.

4. If not serving tarts immediately, refrigerate to chill. Bring to room temperature before serving. Tarts are best enjoyed on the day they are assembled.

Tartlets with Pastry Cream and Mixed Berries

Hazelnut, Raspberry Jam, and
White Chocolate Ganache Tarts

Crostatine con Frolla alla Nocciola, Marmellata di Lamponi, e Crema Ganache al Cioccolato Bianco

Hazelnut, Raspberry Jam, and White Chocolate Ganache Tarts

These tarts use only about two-thirds of the *pasta frolla alle nocciole* recipe. I usually roll out the remaining dough, bake it in tart pans, and then store the baked shells in the freezer for another use. To make these tarts, you'll need eight 4½-inch tart pans with removable bottoms.

uno CREMA GANACHE AL CIOCCOLATO BIANCO (WHITE CHOCOLATE GANACHE)

1¼ cups (250 g) mascarpone cheese

½ cup plus ½ tablespoon (125 ml) heavy cream

8 ounces (226 g) white chocolate, finely chopped

due TART SHELLS

Pasta Frolla alle Nocciole (Hazelnut Sweet Pastry Dough) (page 18)

tre MARMELLATA DI LAMPONI (RASPBERRY JAM)

2½ cups (280 g) fresh or frozen raspberries (defrosting is not necessary)

½ cup (113 g) superfine sugar

3 teaspoons lemon juice

finale ASSEMBLY

½ cup plus ½ tablespoon (125 ml) heavy cream

fresh raspberries, for garnish

uno TO MAKE THE WHITE CHOCOLATE GANACHE

1. In a small saucepan over medium heat, bring the mascarpone cheese and cream to a simmer, stirring constantly until the mascarpone is melted.

2. Place the white chocolate in a medium heatproof bowl. Pour the hot mascarpone mixture over the chocolate and let stand for 2 minutes.

3. Whisk until the chocolate has melted and the mixture is smooth. Cover and refrigerate until completely cool and firm, 2 to 3 hours.

due TO MAKE THE TART SHELLS

1. Lightly knead the pastry dough, and divide the dough in two, making one piece with about two-thirds of the dough and the second piece the remaining third. Shape each piece into a ball and pat each ball into a disk. Wrap each disk in plastic wrap. Refrigerate the larger disk for 1 hour. Store the remaining dough in the freezer according to the recipe instructions.

2. Transfer the pastry dough to a lightly floured work surface and roll out to ⅛ inch thick. Cut the dough into 8 (6-inch) rounds. Fit the rounds into 8 (4½-inch) tart pans with removable bottoms. Trim any extra pastry from the edges with a sharp pastry knife. Pierce the bottoms of the pastry shells with a fork. Transfer to a baking sheet and freeze until firm, about 30 minutes, to prevent the pastry from shrinking when baked.

3. Preheat the oven to 375°F (190°C). Line each tart shell with parchment paper, leaving a 1-inch overhang, and fill with ceramic pie weights, or uncooked beans or rice. Arrange the pans on a baking sheet and blind bake for 15 minutes. Remove from the oven. Remove the weights and paper. Return to the oven to bake for an additional 5 to 10 minutes, or until golden.

4. Remove from the oven and transfer to a wire rack to cool in the pans for 2 to 3 minutes. Remove the shells from the pans and return to the wire rack to cool completely.

tre TO MAKE THE RASPBERRY JAM

1. Preheat the oven to 350°F (180°C).

2. Place the raspberries, sugar, and lemon juice in an ovenproof dish. Toss to coat the berries. Bake until thickened and sticky, 30 to 35 minutes.

3. Transfer the baking dish to wire rack and allow the jam to cool completely.

4. To remove the seeds, pass the jam through a fine-mesh sieve into a small bowl.

5. Transfer the jam to a small jar, cover, and refrigerate until cold.

finale TO ASSEMBLE AND SERVE

1. Whisk the heavy cream until soft peaks form.

2. Remove the white chocolate ganache from the refrigerator. Whisk one-half of the whipped cream into the cold chocolate mixture, then whisk in the remaining whipped cream.

3. Spoon 1 to 2 teaspoons raspberry jam into each cooled pastry shell. Don't add too much, because you do not want the jam to come up the sides when you add the white chocolate ganache. Use the back of a small spoon to spread the jam and completely cover the base of the shell.

4. Divide the ganache among the pastry shells. Use a small offset spatula to spread the filling to the edges of the pastry.

5. Refrigerate the tarts for at least 1 hour. To serve, garnish with fresh raspberries.

Pastries and Fried Desserts

Sicilian Cannoli

Cannoli Siciliani

Sicilian Cannoli

To make these classic Italian pastries, you'll need several special tools: a pasta machine; a 3 by 4½-inch oval or a 3 by ½-inch round cookie cutter; many ¾ by 5½-inch cannoli forms; and a large pastry bag with a large round plain tip (like a Wilton 1A). Note that if you don't have an appropriate cookie cutter, you can make a 3 by 4½-inch oval template from cardboard and cut the dough with a sharp paring knife and pastry wheel. If you don't have a pasta machine, you can roll the dough by hand, bearing in mind that it must be quite thin. To maintain crispy cannoli shells, fill them with *crema di ricotta* immediately before serving.

uno CIALDE PER CANNOLI (CANNOLI SHELLS)

>   vegetable oil, for frying
>
>   1⅓ cups (167 g) all-purpose flour
>
>   ¼ teaspoon salt
>
>   2 teaspoons (5 g) unsweetened cocoa powder (not Dutch processed)
>
>   1 tablespoon (14 g) superfine sugar
>
>   2 tablespoons (28 g) vegetable shortening
>
>   6 to 7 tablespoons sweet marsala wine, as needed
>
>   1 to 2 large egg whites, lightly beaten

finale ASSEMBLY

>   3½ cups Crema di Ricotta (Ricotta Cream) (page 14)
>
>   finely chopped unsalted pistachios (optional)
>
>   maraschino cherries, cut in half (optional)
>
>   confectioners' sugar, sifted, for dusting

uno TO MAKE THE CANNOLI SHELLS

1. Line a rimmed baking sheet with 3 to 4 layers of paper towels (to absorb excess oil). Line a second rimmed baking sheet with parchment paper or a silicone baking mat. Pour 3 to 4 inches of oil into a deep, heavy pot, and attach a thermometer to the side.

2. Using a fine-mesh sieve, sift the flour, salt, and cocoa into the bowl of a stand mixer. Add the sugar. Fit the mixer with the paddle attachment, and stir to combine well.

3. Add the vegetable shortening and beat on low speed until the mixture resembles a fine crumb, 1 to 2 minutes.

4. With the mixer on low speed, gradually add 6 tablespoons of marsala, beating until the pastry dough starts to come together in a ball. If the dough isn't coming together, add the remaining 1 tablespoon marsala a little at a time (you may not need the entire tablespoon).

5. Transfer the dough to a clean work surface and knead it with your hands until smooth, 2 to 3 minutes. (It's not necessary to flour the work surface, in fact, it's best not to.) Shape the dough into a ball, flatten it into a disk, and wrap in plastic. Allow the dough to rest at room temperature for 1 hour.

6. Divide the dough into quarters. Work with one piece of dough at a time and keep the remaining pieces wrapped in plastic. Set the rollers of a hand-crank or electric pasta machine to the widest opening.

7. Flatten the piece of dough and run it through the machine. If the dough is sticky, flour it very lightly (you want to refrain from flouring the dough if at all possible). Fold the dough in thirds (like a business letter), flatten with your fingers and pass through the widest setting again. Repeat this at least 2 more times to knead the dough.

8. Decrease the roller opening by one notch. Without folding the pastry, pass it once through the rollers. Keep rolling the sheet through the machine, decreasing the roller opening each time until you have rolled it through the second to last setting. The pastry should be very thin. (Dust very lightly with flour if necessary.)

9. Transfer the pastry sheet to a covered work surface. If the pastry is sticky, dust both sides very lightly with flour and then cover with a table cloth or kitchen towels. Repeat the kneading and rolling process with the remaining pieces of dough, working with one piece at a time.

10. Heat the oil over high heat to 350°F to 360°F (180°C to 182°C). (If you don't have a thermometer, drop a 1-inch cube of bread into the hot oil. If it takes about 1 minute to brown all sides of the cube and it floats to the top, the oil has reached the appropriate temperature for deep-frying.)

11. Working with one sheet of pastry at a time, place the pastry sheet on a clean work surface, like a cutting board. Using a 3 x 4½-inch oval cookie cutter or a 3½-inch round cookie cutter, cut out rounds of dough. Cover the rounds of dough with a tablecloth or kitchen towels.

12. Very lightly coat the cannoli forms with cooking spray. Working with one round of dough at a time, wrap the pastry around the form. To prevent the pastry from unwrapping from the form when frying, moisten the edge of the pastry with the beaten egg white and press gently to seal. Transfer the pastry-wrapped form to the prepared baking sheet lined with parchment or a silicone baking mat and cover with a kitchen towel. Repeat with the remaining rounds of dough.

13. When oil reaches the correct temperature, fry the cannoli shells. Using tongs, carefully slip 3 to 4 cannoli shells at a time into the hot oil (they will sink). After a couple of seconds, use the tongs to grasp the shells by the tube ends and move them around. The dough will have developed dozens of small bubbles all over the surface.

14. After about 45 seconds, remove the forms by using the tongs to grasp the edge of the forms. Very carefully shake the form to release the shell back into the oil as you pull the form out. If it does not come away on its own, use a butter knife to gently and carefully push one side of the shell to release the shell back into the oil. (If necessary, remove the form from the oil and, over the paper

towel lined-baking sheet, remove the shell by pushing on the shell gently with a butter knife and then carefully transfer the shell back to the hot oil with the tongs.) Transfer the form to the prepared baking sheet lined with paper towels to drain and cool. Be very careful, the tube is extremely hot.

15. Continue to cook the shells until lightly golden, 1 to 2 minutes. Watch them carefully, as the shells darken quickly. You may have to adjust the cooking time as you go. Use the tongs to gently lift each shell out of the oil, draining the oil back into the pot, and transfer the shells to the baking sheet lined with paper towels to drain and cool. Allow the forms to cool completely, then wipe clean with a paper towel. Maintain the oil temperature while the forms cool and you prepare the remaining shells.

16. Repeat the process with the remaining pieces of dough. Depending on how many cannoli forms you have, you may have to cut, wrap, and fry pastry shells in batches. Make sure you allow enough time in between to cool the forms; they will be extremely hot. Usually I take this time to cut my next batch of dough. After frying the first batch of shells, wipe the forms (don't wash them) with a paper towel before wrapping with another pastry round. It is not necessary to grease the forms between batches even after wiping them clean.

17. Allow the cannoli shells to cool completely before filling.

18. Store unfilled cannoli shells between layers of parchment in an airtight container at room temperature for up to 1 week, or frozen up to 1 month.

finale TO ASSEMBLE AND SERVE

1. Just before serving, transfer the ricotta filling to a large pastry bag with fitted large round plain tip (like a Wilton 1A).

2. Working with one pastry shell at a time, insert the pastry tip into one side of the shell and gently squeeze, filling the shell half full. Repeat on the other side of the shell.

3. If using pistachios, smooth the exposed filling on both ends of the cannolo with the back of a small spoon and sprinkle both ends with pistachios. If using maraschino cherries, place one half on the cream at each end of the cannolo.

4. Dust the cannoli with confectioners' sugar and serve immediately.

Piccoli Cialde per Cannoli

Mini Cannoli Shells

To make these small cannoli shells, perfect toppers for Piccoli Torta alla Vaniglia con Crema di Ricotta, Panna Montata al Cacao e Marsala (Cannoli Cupcakes with Marsala-Chocolate Whipped Cream, page 77), you'll need half of the standard cannoli dough recipe (see page 137). I use the remaining dough to bake a half-batch of regular cannoli to enjoy immediately or freeze for a later date. You'll also need a 2¼-inch oval or round cookie cutter, and homemade mini cannoli forms (see sidebar).

vegetable oil, for frying

½ recipe Cialde per Cannoli (Cannoli Shells) (page 137)

1. Line a tray or rimmed baking sheet with parchment paper. The tray should be large enough to accommodate 12 pastry-wrapped mini cannoli forms in a single layer with a small space in between each one. Line a rimmed baking sheet with three to four layers of paper towels. Pour 3 inches of oil in a large, heavy pot. Attach a thermometer to the side of the pot.

2. Prepare the pastry dough for the cannoli shells by following steps 2 to 15 and using 12 homemade mini cannoli forms lightly coated with cooking spray. (With the smaller cannoli it may be necessary to coat the forms with cooking spray each and every time.) Cut the rolled dough out with a 2¼-inch oval or round cookie cutter and wrap each round around a mini cannoli form. Fry the cannoli shells for only seconds before removing the aluminum foil forms. After you've removed the forms, continue to cook the shells until lightly golden, about 30 seconds longer.

TO MAKE HOMEMADE MINI CANNOLI FORMS

Makes 12 forms

1. Cut 24 (6 x 3½-inch) strips of aluminum foil.
2. Stack two strips of foil on a flat surface with the shorter edge closest to you. Set a pencil on top of the foil parallel to the shorter edge.
3. Roll the pencil forward, wrapping the foil tightly around its length as you go.
4. Before removing the pencil, make sure the foil tube is secure (you don't want it to unravel when deep frying).
5. Repeat with the remaining strips.

Cannoncini di Sfolgia con Crema Pasticcera al Cioccolato

Chocolate Pastry Cream–Filled Puff Pastry Horns

Cannoncini di sfolgia are classic delicate Italian pastries. They are probably one of the more requested and enjoyed pastries in Italy, and an Italian pastry tray wouldn't be complete without them. To make the pastry horns, buttery strips of puff pastry are wrapped around cream horn molds. When baked, the layers expand to puffy, crispy, and flavorful shells. Traditionally the horns are filled with *crema pasticcera* (pastry cream), but there are many variations. This recipe fills them with *crema pasticcera al cioccolato* (chocolate pastry cream). They are often decorated with chopped, toasted nuts, icing sugar, coarse sugar, vanilla sugar, and melted chocolate. For a simpler, classic variation, and my favorite one, brush the pastry with milk and sprinkle with sanding sugar just before baking. When the horns are cool, fill with plain Crema Pasticcera (page 10).

When making *cannoncini*, be sure that the pastry is extremely cold, otherwise the strips will tear when winding around the molds. You'll also need a hot oven for the pastry horns to expand. To keep their crispy texture, the horns should not be filled until immediately before serving, otherwise they will become soggy.

uno CANNONCINI DI SFOGLIA (PASTRY HORNS)

2 (10 x 10-inch) sheets (450 g) store-bought frozen puff pastry, thawed in the refrigerator or homemade Pasta Sfoglia (page 22)

vegetable spray, for greasing

flour, for dusting

confectioners' sugar, for dusting

finale ASSEMBLY

3 cups Crema Pasticcera al Cioccolato (Chocolate Pastry Cream) (page 11)

1 cup plus 1 tablespoon (250 ml) heavy cream

4 ounces (113 g) good-quality chocolate, milk, semisweet, or bittersweet, melted and slightly cooled

⅓ cup (50 g) toasted hazelnuts (see page 20)

⅓ cup (50 g) toasted pistachios, finely chopped (see page 20)

⅓ cup (50 g) toasted almonds, finely chopped (see page 20)

uno TO MAKE THE PASTRY HORNS

1. Line 4 baking sheets with parchment paper or silicone baking mats. Lightly grease 40 (or as many as you have to a maximum of 40) cream horn molds with cooking spray. You may have to prepare horns in batches depending on how many molds you have.

2. Lay one sheet of puff pastry on a lightly floured work surface. Keep the remaining puff pastry in the refrigerator. Lightly dust the pastry with flour.

3. Using a pastry wheel or the tip of a sharp knife, cut the pastry sheet into ½-inch ribbons. If using a knife, cut in one clean motion rather than a sawing motion. If using the wheel, roll in one direction rather than back and forth, otherwise it will pinch the layers of pastry and prevent them from expanding.

4. Beginning at the tip of a mold, wind a pastry ribbon around the cone, starting from the pointed end and working toward the wide end, overlapping the layers of pastry slightly to cover the mold. To prevent the pastry from unraveling, secure it at the wide end with a dab of water, making sure to secure pastry to pastry rather than pastry to mold. Transfer the pastry-wrapped mold to a prepared baking sheets. Cover with a kitchen towel to prevent drying out. Repeat with the remaining strips. Transfer the pastry-wrapped molds to the freezer to chill for 30 minutes.

5. Repeat with the remaining sheet of puff pastry. You should have 10 molds per baking sheet.

6. Preheat the oven to 400°F (200°C).

7. Bake one sheet of pastry horns at a time. Just before baking, remove from the freezer and dust with confectioners' sugar. Using a spray bottle filled with water, lightly spritz the pastry just before sliding the baking sheet into the oven. The water creates steam, which helps to expand the layers of pastry.

8. Bake until golden, 18 to 20 minutes. Do not open oven door in the first 15 minutes of baking.

9. Remove from the oven, transfer the pastry horns to a wire rack, and let cool on the molds until cool enough to handle. Carefully remove the pastry from the molds and transfer directly to the wire rack to cool completely.

10. Repeat with the remaining pastry horns.

finale TO ASSEMBLE

1. Prepare the chocolate pastry cream according to the recipe directions, but replace half the milk (1 cup plus 1 tablespoon, or 250 ml) with heavy cream. If it was prepared in advance and refrigerated, be sure to bring to room temperature and give it a whisk to return it to a smooth, creamy consistency before filling the pastry horns.

2. Line a rimmed baking sheet with parchment paper. Working with one pastry horn at a time, dip the tip of the horn into the melted chocolate, allowing any excess to drip off. Roll the chocolate in the chopped hazelnuts, pistachios, or almonds, and set on the prepared baking sheet. Repeat with the remaining horns.

3. Refrigerate the horns to set the chocolate prior to filling, 10 to 15 minutes. Do not fill until the chocolate is set or you may have difficulty piping the pastry cream.

4. Transfer the chocolate pastry cream to a large pastry bag fitted with a large decorative tip (like a Wilton 1M).

5. Insert the pastry tip into a pastry horn and pipe it full of chocolate pastry cream. Repeat with the remaining horns. Serve immediately.

Chocolate-Filled Pastry Horns

Cicerchiata-Struffoli

SERVES 8 TO 10 (MAKES 1 LARGE BOWL OR WREATH)

Italian Honey Balls

Cicerciata is a traditional Abruzzi dessert found in almost every home around *Carnevale* (carnival or Mardi Gras). These balls of fried dough coated in honey syrup immediately transport me back to my childhood. In fact, the word *cicerchiata* is said to come from the dessert's resemblance to chickpeas and the Italian word for chickpeas is *ceci*. While the *cicerchiata* are often topped with chopped almonds, candied fruit, and candy sprinkles, my favorite way to enjoy them is simply coated in melted honey.

6 large eggs

¼ teaspoon salt

3 cups (375 g) all-purpose flour

canola or vegetable oil, for frying

3 cups (710 ml) honey

½ cup (75 g) finely diced candied fruit like glacéed cherries, candied citron, candied orange peel (optional)

50 g (⅓ cup) slivered almonds (optional)

candy sprinkles (optional)

cooking spray (if shaping into a wreath)

1. Crack the eggs into a small bowl, cover with plastic wrap, and allow to come to room temperature, about 30 minutes.

2. Add the salt to the eggs and lightly beat with a fork.

3. Place the flour on a work surface or in a large bowl. Make a well in the center.

4. Pour the egg mixture into the center of the well. With your fingertips or a fork, gradually draw the flour into the egg mixture. Continue until all or most of the flour is incorporated.

5. Use your hands to gather the dough together. Knead until smooth and no longer sticky, 5 to 7 minutes.

6. Shape the dough into a ball, cover with an overturned bowl or kitchen towel, or wrap in plastic. Let the dough rest at room temperature for 30 minutes.

7. Fill a large, heavy sauté pan or skillet with 2 inches of oil. Attach a thermometer to the pan and heat the oil over medium heat to between 365°F and 370°F (185°C and 190°C). (If you don't have a thermometer, drop a 1-inch cube of bread into the hot oil. If it takes about 1 minute to brown all sides of the cube and it floats to the top, the oil has reached the appropriate temperature for frying.)

8. Line a rimmed baking sheet with 3 to 4 layers of paper towels. Line a second rimmed baking sheet with parchment paper or a silicone baking mat.

9. Knead the rested dough for 2 minutes.

10. Cut the dough into 12 equal pieces. Work with one piece of dough at a time, keeping the remaining dough covered. Using your palms to roll each piece of dough into a rope ½ inch thick. Cut the rope

into ¼-inch or ½-inch pieces. (The balls of dough puff out quite a bit when frying. If I am making a wreath, I prefer to cut the dough into smaller pieces. You may want to fry a small batch before cutting all the dough to see which size you prefer.) Transfer the dough pieces to the prepared baking sheet lined with parchment paper and cover with a kitchen towel to prevent the dough from drying out.

11. Fry the dough pieces in small batches (do not overcrowd the pan), stirring occasionally with a slotted spoon, until lightly golden on all sides, 1½ to 3 minutes, depending on the size of the pieces.

12. Using a slotted spoon, transfer the fried balls of dough to the baking sheet lined with paper towels.

13. When all dough is fried, allow the dough balls to come to room temperature.

14. Meanwhile, in a medium saucepan over low heat, bring the honey to a simmer, stirring occasionally, until melted.

15. Transfer the dough balls to a large bowl. If shaping into a wreath, reserve ¼ cup of the melted honey. Pour the remaining honey over the dough balls, stirring with a wooden spoon until well incorporated.

16. If shaping the honey balls into a wreath, reserve a portion of the candied fruit, nuts, or sprinkles (or all three), if using. Sprinkle the remaining fruit, nuts, or sprinkles over the top of the honey balls and stir to combine well.

17. To serve, spoon into a bowl, pile onto a serving dish, or shape into a wreath.

18. To shape into a wreath, coat the outside of a round ramekin, custard cup, or glass with cooking spray. Place in the center of a large platter.

19. Using a large spoon, arrange the honey balls around the ramekin, cup, or glass to form a wreath shape. Allow the wreath to set at room temperature, 2 to 3 hours.

20. Remove the ramekin, cup, or glass from the center of the wreath.

21. Reheat the reserved honey and drizzle over the wreath. Decorate with the reserved candied fruit, nuts, or sprinkles, if using.

Italian Honey Balls

Profiteroles with Chantilly Cream

Bignè alla Crema Chantilly

Profiteroles with Chantilly Cream

Where did the *bignè* originate? If you ask the Italians, you'll probably receive a different answer than if you ask the French, although both think the recipe was created during the Renaissance. The Italians believe that when Caterina de Medici, an Italian noblewoman from Tuscany, moved to France in 1533 to marry Henry II, she brought all of her personal recipes and chefs with her. It's believed that one of the chefs created the recipe for *bignè* in 1540. It's also thought that not only the recipe for *bignè* but also many of the basic pastry recipes that France is famous for today would have been credited to the Italians had de Medici remained in Italy. *Bignè* are best served on the day they are made. If necessary, they can be baked up to two days before serving and should be reheated in a preheated 350°F (180°C) oven until crispy, 3 to 5 minutes. To prevent the *bignè* from going soggy, fill just before serving.

1½ pounds (680 g) Pasta Choux (Choux Pastry) (page 26)

4½ cups Crema Chantilly (Chantilly Cream) (page 12)

1. Preheat the oven to 425°F (220°C). Line 2 rimmed baking sheets with parchment paper or silicone baking mats.

2. Transfer the choux pastry to a large pastry bag fitted with ½-inch plain tip (like Wilton 1A). For larger profiteroles, pipe the paste into 1½-inch rounds, spacing 3 inches apart on the prepared baking sheets. For smaller profiteroles, pipe the paste into 1-inch rounds, about 1 inch in diameter, spacing 2 inches apart on the prepared baking sheets. To prevent the tops from burning, level the peaks with a wet fingertip.

3. Bake one sheet of profiteroles at a time. Using a small spray bottle filled with water, lightly spritz the profiteroles with water and immediately place in the oven. The water will help to create steam, which helps give the profiteroles volume.

4. Bake until tops and sides are golden, 25 to 30 minutes for larger profiteroles and 15 to 20 minutes for smaller ones. Turn off the oven and allow to rest in the oven for 5 minutes.

5. Remove from the oven. Pierce each profiterole in the side with a small paring knife to allow steam to escape. Transfer to a wire rack and allow to cool completely.

6. With a serrated knife, cut each profiterole in half crosswise.

8. Transfer the chantilly cream to a large piping bag fitted with a large tip (like a Wilton 1M). Pipe the cream in a decorative swirl on the bottom half of each profiteroles. Replace the tops.

9. To serve, dust with confectioners' sugar. If not serving immediately, filled profiteroles can be stored in an airtight container in the refrigerator for up to two hours (any longer could cause the pastry to go soggy).

Chocolate Éclairs with Pastry Cream

Èclairs al Cioccolato con Crema Pasticcera

MAKES 24 ÉCLAIRS

Chocolate Éclairs with Pastry Cream

uno ÉCLAIR BUNS

1½ pounds Pasta Choux (Choux Pastry) (page 26)

due ÉCLAIR FILLING

3 cups Crema Pasticcera 2 (Page 11)

1 vanilla bean

tre CREMA GANACHE (CHOCOLATE GANACHE GLAZE)

4 ounces (113 g) semisweet chocolate, finely chopped

½ cup (120 ml) heavy cream

1 tablespoon light corn syrup

uno TO MAKE THE ÉCLAIR BUNS

1. Preheat the oven to 425°F (220°C). Line 2 rimmed baking sheets with parchment paper or silicone baking mats.

2. Transfer the choux pastry to a large pastry bag fitted with plain tip with a ½-inch opening (like a Wilton 1A). Pipe the paste into logs 4½ inches long, spacing 2 inches apart onto the prepared baking sheets.

3. Bake one sheet of buns at a time. Using a spray bottle filled with water, spritz the buns lightly and immediately place in the oven. Bake until tops and sides are golden, 25 to 30 minutes. Turn off the oven and allow to rest in the oven for 5 minutes.

4. Remove from the oven. Pierce each bun on each end with a small paring knife to release the steam. Transfer to a wire rack to cool completely.

5. While the buns cool, prepare the pastry cream and chocolate ganache.

due TO MAKE THE ÉCLAIR FILLING

1. Prepare the pastry cream according to the recipe directions, but use only 6 egg yolks and use 2 vanilla beans (the extra bean is optional, but will give the éclair a wonderful vanilla flavor). Refrigerate until ready to fill the buns.

PASTRIES AND FRIED DESSERTS 149

tre TO MAKE THE CHOCOLATE GANACHE GLAZE

1. Place the chocolate in small heatproof bowl.

2. In a small saucepan over medium heat, bring the cream just to a simmer.

3. Remove from the heat. Add the corn syrup and whisk to combine.

4. Pour the cream mixture over the chocolate. Let stand, without stirring, until the chocolate begins to melt, about 2 minutes.

5. Using small flexible spatula, stir the chocolate and cream together. Begin near the center of the bowl and gradually work your way toward the edge, pulling in as much chocolate as possible, until the glaze is smooth, glossy, and well combined.

6. Strain the glaze through a fine-mesh sieve into a small bowl (discard any solids).

7. If not using immediately, the glaze can be stored in an airtight container in the refrigerator for 5 days. Gently reheat before using.

finale TO ASSEMBLE

1. Working with one bun at a time, insert a wooden skewer into one end of the bun and move the skewer around to expand the opening to make room for the filling. Repeat on the other end. (Alternatively, cut each bun in half with a serrated knife.)

2. Remove the pastry cream from the refrigerator and whisk until smooth. (If you cut the buns in half, don't whisk the cream, or it may become too soft to pipe.)

3. Transfer the pastry cream to a large pastry bag fitted with a small plain tip.

4. Working with one bun at a time, insert the pastry tip into one end of the bun. Gently squeeze the filling until the bun is half full. Repeat with the other side of the bun. Repeat with the remaining buns. (If you cut the buns in half, using a decorative tip with a ½-inch opening, pipe the cream onto the bottom half of each bun. Do not replace the top.)

5. Dip the top of each bun into the ganache, allowing the excess to drip off before turning the éclair over. (If you cut the buns in half, dip the tops in ganache then replace them on the bottoms.) Transfer to a wire rack to allow the ganache to set.

6. Éclairs are at their best when served on the day they are made. They can be stored in an airtight container in the refrigerator for up to 1 day.

Bomboloni alla Crema

Italian Cream-Filled Doughnuts

Bomboloni, sometimes referred to as *bombe fritte*, are Italian doughnuts filled with pastry cream. The *bombolone* (singular) has a distinct look: It's golden on both sides with a band lighter in color in the middle. Although similar to other doughnuts, like the *Berliner* in Germany and the *Krapfen* in Austria, it is filled from the top rather than the side. The traditional filling is pastry cream, but there are variations with jam or chocolate. The dough is often flavored with vanilla and citrus, orange, lemon, or a combination.

uno DOUGHNUTS

2 cups (250 g) bread flour

2 cups (250 g) Italian 00 (doppio zero) flour (see page 8) or all-purpose flour

3½ tablespoons (50 g) superfine sugar, plus more for rolling the doughnuts

1 package (8 g) quick-rise yeast

seeds of 1 vanilla bean

grated zest of 1 orange or lemon

pinch of salt

1 cup plus 1 tablespoon (250 ml) warm whole milk, between 105 and 110°F (40 and 43°C)

3 large eggs

3½ tablespoons (50 g) unsalted butter, cut into 4 pieces, softened

vegetable spray, for greasing the pan

vegetable or canola oil, for frying

finale ASSEMBLY

3 cups cooled Crema Pasticcera (Pastry Cream) (page 10)

uno TO MAKE THE DOUGHNUTS

1. In a large bowl, whisk the bread flour, 00 or all-purpose flour, sugar, instant yeast, vanilla bean seeds, orange or lemon zest, and salt until well combined.

2. Make a well in the center of the flour mixture and pour in the warm milk. Work together the milk and the flour mixture with the tips of your fingers.

3. Add the eggs all at once, and work the ingredients together until you have a rough ball of dough.

4. Add the butter one piece at a time, working each piece of butter into the dough before adding the next.

5. Transfer the dough to a lightly floured work surface and knead until smooth and elastic, 10 to 15 minutes.

6. Transfer dough back to the large bowl. Cover with a sheet of plastic wrap and leave to rise in a warm place, 1½ to 2 hours.

7. Cut 32 (4-inch) square sheets of parchment. Line three 3-inch-deep baking dishes with the parchment squares and lightly spray with cooking spray. (You can also use rimmed baking sheets; I like the deep dish because it ensures that when the dough rises again, the tops of the doughnuts won't stick to the plastic wrap.)

8. When the dough has doubled in volume, transfer to a lightly floured work surface. Roll the dough out to a thickness of a little less than ½-inch. Use a 2-¾ to 3-inch round cookie cutter or drinking glass to cut out rounds of dough; keep the cuts as close together as possible. Transfer and center each round onto a prepared parchment square (centering the doughnut allows for the size once the dough has risen) on the prepared baking sheet. Cover the rounds of dough with plastic wrap and leave to rise in a warm place until doubled in volume, 1½ to 2 hours; they should appear full of air.

9. Gather up the leftover pieces and give the dough a quick knead to bring the pieces back together. Return the dough to the bowl, cover with plastic wrap, and leave to rise in a warm place until doubled in volume, about 30 minutes. Roll out the dough again and cut more rounds. At this point if you have any remaining dough, gather it together, re-roll, and cut rounds until all of the dough has been used.

10. Cover the remaining rounds of dough with plastic wrap and leave to rise in a warm place until doubled in volume, 1½ to 2 hours; they should appear full of air. Keep these doughnuts separate from the doughnuts you cut first, because they will not be ready for frying at the same time as the first cut dough rounds.

finale TO ASSEMBLE

1. Fill a large, heavy 6-quart (6 liter) saucepan with 3½ inches of oil. Heat the oil over medium heat to 320°F to 340°F (160°C to 170°C), about 20 minutes. (Check the oil frequently while frying the doughnuts to maintain the temperature. If you have a thermometer, attach it to the saucepan to monitor the temperature of the oil.) Layer one large plate with three to four sheets of paper towels for draining the fried doughnuts. Cover a second large plate with a thin layer of superfine sugar, for rolling the doughnuts.

2. When the oil is hot, fry four to six doughnuts at a time to ensure even frying. Begin frying the first batch of cut doughnuts. The remaining doughnuts should be ready once the first batch is fried. Carefully lift the doughnuts up off the baking dish by grasping 2 opposite corners of the baking paper. When placing the doughnuts in the oil, place them with the parchment squares, within seconds of frying the paper will easily slip away and can be removed with tongs. (This method of allowing the doughnuts to rise on the squares and then placing in the oil with the papers reduces the amount of handling of the dough, preventing the chance of knocking out any air, which of course translates to lighter, airier doughnuts.) Fry until golden on both sides, 3 to 5 minutes total. (The doughnuts should be golden on both sides, with a distinct lighter-colored line in the middle. This can be difficult to achieve at times because the doughnuts have a mind of their own and they puff up while cooking, sometimes more on one side than the other.) With a spider skimmer or slotted

spoon, remove the fried doughnuts one at a time. Drain on the paper towels and immediately roll in the superfine sugar until evenly coated.

3. Transfer the pastry cream to a large pastry bag fitted with a ¼ to ½-inch plain round tip. While the doughnuts are still warm, use a sharp paring knife to make a small hole in the top center of each doughnut. Insert the pastry tip into the hole and pipe the pastry cream until the doughnut feels heavy; continue to fill until there is a mound of pastry cream on top. Repeat with the remaining doughnuts.

4. Doughnuts are best enjoyed on the day they are made. Serve immediately.

Italian Cream-Filled Doughnuts

Panini di Sfoglia con Cioccolato

Chocolate Croissants

If life is hectic and you don't have the time to make homemade pastry, don't let that hold you back from enjoying *panini di cioccolato*. Simply use store-bought puff pastry instead. And if you buy the pastry that has two sheets per package, that's all the better because the sheets are the perfect size—10-inch square. You'll need two packages for this recipe. For the chocolate, I find that 3½ x 7½-inch good-quality chocolate bars work well.

> *1 recipe Pasta Sfoglia Brioche per Cornetto (Croissant Dough) (page 24) or 2 packages store-bought puff pastry*
>
> *14 ounces (395 g) good-quality semisweet or bittersweet chocolate, cut into 1 x 3-inch sticks*
>
> *1 large egg, lightly beaten, for egg wash*

1. If using store-bought puff pastry, defrost at room temperature for 2 hours or in the refrigerator overnight.

2. Line 2 rimmed baking sheets with parchment paper.

3. Transfer the cold puff pastry dough to a lightly floured work surface. Lightly dust the top of the dough and your rolling pin with flour, and then roll the dough into a 20-inch square.

4. Using a pastry wheel and ruler, cut the dough into 4 (10-inch) squares.

5. Cut each square into thirds to make a total of 12 rectangles measuring about 10 x 3¼ inches.

6. Form the croissants one at a time. Working from the narrow end of a rectangle, lay one chocolate piece on top of the dough about 1½ inches from the edge. Lift the edge of the dough up and over the chocolate piece and seal the edge with your fingertips. Place a second chocolate piece on the sealed edge, then fold over so that the chocolate piece is covered. Continue to fold to the end of the rectangle, making sure there is enough dough remaining to fold under the croissant. (If you get to the end and there's not enough dough to fold underneath, unroll the dough slightly and stretch the end a bit to create a longer rectangle.) Transfer the croissant, seam-side down, to a prepared baking sheet. Repeat with the remaining dough rectangles. You should have 6 croissants per baking sheet, spaced 2 to 3 inches apart.

7. Cover the croissants loosely with parchment paper and let them rise at room temperature until puffy (they will not double in size), 45 to 60 minutes.

8. To bake the croissants, position an oven rack in the middle of the oven. Preheat the oven to 400°F (200°C). Bake one sheet of croissants at a time.

9. Just before baking, brush the surface of each panino with the egg wash. Using a spray bottle filled with cold water, spritz the panini and bake immediately until golden, 18 to 22 minutes, rotating the baking sheet once halfway through.

10. Remove from the oven and transfer to a wire rack. Cool until warm, about 15 minutes. Serve warm or room temperature. Panini are best enjoyed on the day they are made. Store in an airtight container at room temperature.

Creams, Custards, Mousses, and Soufflés

Bavarese alle Fragole

Strawberry Bavarian Cream

La crema bavarese (bavarian cream), or *bavarese* (bavarian), is a classic chilled dessert. Although these are individual servings, the bavarian can also be served as a cake in an 8-inch ring mold or fluted mold. Serve by the slice with fresh fruit and a drizzle of coulis. If using silicone molds, it is best to chill the filled mold in the freezer until firm, making it easier to remove.

uno CREMA BAVARESE (BAVARIAN CREAM)

5 sheets (8⅓ g) unflavored gold gelatin sheets

2⅔ cups (384 g) strawberries, hulled and quartered, plus more for garnish

¾ cup plus 1½ tablespoons (200 ml) whole milk

grated zest of half a lemon

1 vanilla bean, split and seeded

1 tablespoon lemon juice

½ cup (113 g) superfine sugar

¾ cup plus 1½ tablespoons (200 ml) heavy cream

½ cup plus 1½ tablespoons (75 g) confectioners' sugar

due COULIS DI LAMPONI (STRAWBERRY COULIS)

1¼ cups (252 g) strawberries, hulled and quartered

2 tablespoons (30 g) superfine sugar

2 tablespoons (30 ml) water

½ tablespoon orange juice

½ teaspoon grated orange zest

¼ teaspoon pure vanilla extract

½ tablespoon liqueur (such as Grand Marnier or Cointreau)

finale ASSEMBLY

fresh strawberries, for garnish

Sweetened Whipped Cream (page 13), for garnish

uno TO MAKE THE BAVARIAN CREAM

1. Soak the gelatin leaves in a bowl of cold water until softened, about 15 minutes.

2. In a small saucepan, stir together the milk, lemon zest, and the vanilla bean and seeds, and warm over low heat. Remove from the heat just as small bubbles start to form along the sides of the pan. Set aside to cool for 2 minutes.

3. Meanwhile, in a food processor, use a wooden spoon to stir together the strawberries, lemon juice, and sugar. Set aside to macerate for 5 to 7 minutes.

4. Squeeze out the excess liquid from the softened gelatin sheets. Add the sheets to the warm milk mixture and stir to dissolve. Set aside to cool.

5. In a food processor, purée the macerated strawberry mixture. Strain the purée through a fine-mesh sieve into a large bowl (discard the solids).

6. Strain the cooled milk mixture through a fine-mesh sieve into the strawberry purée (discard the solids) and stir until well combined. Let stand until the mixture cools to room temperature.

7. In a medium bowl, use a handheld mixer at high speed to beat the heavy cream and confectioners' sugar to soft peaks.

8. Fold one-third of the whipped cream into strawberry mixture, then fold in the remaining whipped cream until the mixture is smooth.

9. To remove any remaining seeds, strain the mixture through a fine-mesh sieve into a pourable container.

10. Pour the mixture into 6 (6-ounce) molds or 8 (4½-ounce) molds. Chill in the refrigerator until set, 4 to 6 hours, or preferably overnight.

11. If using silicone molds, transfer the molds to the freezer once the bavarian has set to chill until firm.

due TO MAKE THE STRAWBERRY COULIS

1. Place the strawberries, sugar, water, orange juice and zest, and vanilla in a small saucepan. Bring to a simmer over low heat and cook until the berries are soft, 5 to 7 minutes.

2. Remove from the heat and set aside to cool for a few minutes.

3. Transfer the strawberry mixture to a blender or food processor and purée.

4. Strain the purée through a fine-mesh sieve into a small bowl. Cover and refrigerate until completely chilled, about 1½ hours.

5. Stir the liqueur into the cold coulis.

finale TO SERVE

1. If using silicone molds, remove the molds from the freezer and turn out each bavarian onto a dessert dish. Refrigerate to thaw before serving.

2. If using ramekins or custard cups, dip the base of each cup in hot water, wipe dry with a kitchen towel, and run a knife around the inside of each cup. Turn out each bavarian onto a dessert plate.

3. To serve, top with strawberry coulis, fresh strawberries, and a dollop of whipped cream.

Strawberry Bavarian Cream

Panna Cotta con Gelatina di Lamponi SERVES 8

Panna Cotta with Raspberry Jelly

uno PANNA COTTA

    3½ cups (830 ml) whole milk

    1 cup (240 ml) heavy cream

    ¾ cup (169 g) superfine sugar

    1 vanilla bean, split and seeded

    2 tablespoons unflavored powdered gelatin

    ⅓ cup (80 ml) cold water

due GELATINA DI LAMPONI (RASPBERRY JELLY)

    3 cups (420 g) frozen raspberries

    ⅔ cup plus 1 tablespoon (160 g) superfine sugar

    2 teaspoons lime juice (optional)

    1 tablespoon unflavored powdered gelatin

    ⅓ cup (80 ml) cold water

finale ASSEMBLY

    fresh raspberries, for garnish

    fresh mint, for garnish

uno TO MAKE THE PANNA COTTA

1. In a medium saucepan over medium heat, bring the milk, cream, sugar, and the vanilla bean and seeds to a simmer, stirring until the sugar dissolves. Remove from the heat, cover, and allow vanilla to steep, 20 to 30 minutes.

2. To prepare an ice water bath, half fill a large bowl with ice and cover the ice with cold water.

3. Sprinkle the gelatin over the ⅓ cup cold water in a small bowl. Set aside to bloom, about 5 minutes.

4. Meanwhile, reheat the milk mixture over low heat until warmed through.

5. Add the bloomed gelatin to the milk mixture and stir to dissolve completely, about 5 minutes.

6. Pour the milk mixture through a fine-mesh sieve into a medium heatproof bowl. Set the bowl in the ice water bath and stir occasionally until cool but not set, 5 to 10 minutes. Remove from the ice water bath.

7. Spoon the panna cotta evenly among 8 dessert cups. Refrigerate to set, 2 to 4 hours. While the panna cotta sets, prepare the jelly.

due TO MAKE THE RASPBERRY JELLY

1. In a medium saucepan over medium heat, bring the raspberries, sugar, and lime juice, if using, to a boil. Reduce the heat and simmer until the raspberries are soft and have released their juices, about 10 minutes. Remove from the heat.

2. Press the raspberry mixture through a fine-mesh sieve into a large liquid measuring cup (discard the solids). You'll need 2½ cups (590 ml) juice. If there isn't enough juice, top up with water.

3. Sprinkle the gelatin over the cold water in a small bowl. Set aside to bloom, about 5 minutes.

4. Meanwhile, transfer the raspberry juice to a small saucepan over low heat until warmed through.

5. Add the bloomed gelatin and stir to dissolve completely. Remove from the heat and strain the jelly through a fine-mesh sieve into a pourable container. Set aside to cool slightly, stirring occasionally.

6. Pour the jelly evenly among the dessert cups over the panna cotta. Refrigerate to set, about 1 hour.

finale TO ASSEMBLE AND SERVE

1. To serve, top each panna cotta with fresh raspberries and a sprig of mint.

Panna Cotta and Raspberry Jelly

Vanilla Bean Rice Pudding with Peaches, Blueberries, and Amaretto

Budino di Riso alla Vaniglia con Pesche, Mirtilli, e Amaretto

SERVES 4 TO 6

Vanilla Bean Rice Pudding with Peaches, Blueberries, and Amaretto

2½ cups (590 ml) whole milk

½ cup (120 ml) heavy cream

½ cup (100 g) arborio rice

1 vanilla bean, split and seeded

⅓ cup (70 g) superfine sugar

1 tablespoon (15 ml) amaretto

1 teaspoon grated lemon zest

ripe peaches, thinly sliced, to serve

blueberries, to serve

chopped almonds, to serve

honey, to serve

1. In a medium, heavy saucepan, stir together the milk, cream, rice, and the vanilla bean and seeds. Bring to a boil over medium-high heat.

2. Reduce the heat to medium-low and simmer, stirring frequently, until the rice is tender, 20 to 25 minutes.

3. Add the sugar, amaretto, and lemon zest. Cook until the pudding thickens, 5 to 10 minutes.

4. Remove from the heat and discard the vanilla bean.

5. To serve, spoon rice pudding into bowls and top with peach slices, blueberries, chopped almonds, and a drizzle of honey.

CREAMS, CUSTARDS, MOUSSES, AND SOUFFLÉS *163*

Vasetti di Crema alla Vaniglia con Coulis di Lamponi

Vanilla Cream with Raspberry Coulis

uno CREMA ALLA VANIGLIA (VANILLA CREAM)

1⅓ cup plus 2 teaspoons (325 ml) heavy cream

1 cup plus 1 tablespoon (250 ml) whole milk

⅓ cup (80 g) superfine sugar

1 vanilla bean, split and seeded

1 tablespoon cornstarch, sifted

due COULIS DI LAMPONI (RASPBERRY COULIS)

⅓ cup (80 ml) water

2 tablespoons (30 g) superfine sugar

1¾ cups (215 g) raspberries

¼ teaspoon pure vanilla extract

½ tablespoon crème de cassis

1 teaspoon grated orange zest

finale ASSEMBLY

fresh raspberries, for garnish

uno TO MAKE THE VANILLA CREAM

1. In a small saucepan over medium heat, bring the cream, milk, sugar, and the vanilla bean and seeds just to a boil. Remove from the heat, cover, and allow to steep for 20 minutes.

2. Return the pan to low heat.

3. Place the cornstarch in a pourable liquid measuring cup. Add 7 tablespoons (about 105 ml) warm cream mixture and stir with a fork until smooth and the cornstarch is dissolved.

4. Pour the cornstarch mixture in a steady stream through a small fine-mesh sieve into the cream mixture, stirring constantly. Bring the cream back to a boil over low heat and cook until thickened, 3 to 5 minutes.

5. Remove from the heat. Transfer the mixture to small bowl and place a sheet of plastic wrap directly onto the cream to prevent a skin from forming while it cools, about 30 minutes. Occasionally remove the plastic wrap and give the cream a stir.

6. Once cool, spoon the cream into 4 (4-ounce) serving cups, leaving enough room for the coulis, and refrigerate to cool completely, about 1 hour.

due TO MAKE THE RASPBERRY COULIS

1. In a small saucepan, bring the water, sugar, raspberries, and vanilla to a simmer over low heat and simmer until the sugar is dissolved and the raspberries have softened, 3 to 4 minutes.

2. Remove from the heat and stir in the crème de cassis and orange zest. Cool slightly.

3. Pour the raspberry mixture into a blender or food processor and purée.

4. Strain the purée through a fine-mesh sieve into a small bowl (discard the solids). Set aside to cool.

5. Refrigerate until cold.

finale TO SERVE

1. To serve, spoon the cold coulis over the vanilla cream and top with fresh raspberries.

Vanilla Cream with Raspberry Coulis

Dark and White Chocolate Mousse

Mousse al Cioccolato Fondente e Mousse al Cioccolato Bianco

Dark and White Chocolate Mousse

I immediately turn to a mousse dessert when I'm hosting a large dinner party. Because all the elements of this dessert can be prepared ahead and plated in mere minutes, it allows me to enjoy time with my guests rather than spending the evening in the kitchen. The mousse keeps very well in the freezer for a couple weeks. It thaws in the refrigerator in no time at all.

To make this, you'll need ⅓-cup half-sphere silicone molds and 16 (1 x 4½-inch) acetate tubes. To make the acetate tubes, cut acetate into 16 (3¾ x 4½ inch) rectangles. Wrap each rectangle around a 1-inch tube so the ends overlap and secure with tape. Cover one end of each tube with plastic wrap and secure with tape. For a simpler version, layer the mousse in glasses and top with chocolate sauce and berry coulis.

uno MOUSSE AL CIOCCOLATO FONDENTE (DARK CHOCOLATE MOUSSE)

- 12 ounces (340 g) good-quality bittersweet chocolate, 60%, finely chopped
- 2 tablespoons (30 ml) dark rum
- 1 teaspoon pure vanilla extract
- ¼ cup plus 2 tablespoons (84 g) superfine sugar
- 2 tablespoons (30 ml) water
- 5 large egg yolks, at room temperature
- 2 cups (475 ml) cold heavy cream

due MOUSSE AL CIOCCOLATO BIANCO (WHITE CHOCOLATE MOUSSE)

- 4 sheets (6⅔ g) gold gelatin sheets
- 12 ounces good-quality white chocolate, finely chopped
- 1 teaspoon pure vanilla extract
- 3 tablespoons (42 g) superfine sugar
- 1 tablespoon (15 ml) water
- 5 large egg yolks, at room temperature
- 1 large egg white, at room temperature
- 3 tablespoons whole milk
- 2 cups (475 ml) cold heavy cream

tre SALSA DI FRAGOLE E LAMPONI (STRAWBERRY-RASPBERRY COULIS)

- 1 cup (149 g) fresh or frozen strawberries, hulled and sliced
- 1 cup (140 g) fresh or frozen raspberries
- ¼ cup (57 g) superfine sugar
- 2 tablespoons (30 ml) orange juice
- 1 teaspoon grated orange zest
- ½ tablespoon rum

quattro SALSA AL CIOCCOLATO (CHOCOLATE SAUCE)

>*8 ounces (226 g) good-quality bittersweet chocolate, 60%, finely chopped*
>
>*½ cup (120 ml) heavy cream*
>
>*3 tablespoons (42 g) superfine sugar*
>
>*1 teaspoon pure vanilla extract*
>
>*1 tablespoon (15 ml) rum*
>
>*1 tablespoon (14 g) unsalted butter*

finale TO ASSEMBLE

>*fresh raspberries*
>
>*fresh strawberries*
>
>*biscotti or amaretti cookies*

uno TO MAKE THE DARK CHOCOLATE MOUSSE

1. Melt the chocolate in a medium heatproof bowl over a saucepan of just-simmering water over low heat, stirring occasionally, until smooth (do not let the bowl touch the water). Remove from the heat, stir in the rum and vanilla, and set aside to cool.

2. In a small saucepan over medium heat, stir together the sugar and water until the sugar dissolves. Attach a candy thermometer to the side of the pan and continue to cook the sugar without stirring until the syrup reaches 243°F (118°C).

3. Meanwhile, in a medium bowl, use a handheld mixer to beat the egg yolks at high speed.

4. When the sugar syrup reaches the correct temperature, continue to beat the egg yolks while slowly pouring the syrup in a steady stream down the side of the bowl; make sure the syrup does not come in contact with the beaters. Continue to beat the mixture until it is almost white in color and it cools to a temperature of 85°F (29°C).

5. Whisk the melted chocolate into the egg mixture.

6. In a stand mixer fitted with the whip attachment, beat the heavy cream at high speed to soft peaks, about 2 minutes.

7. Whisk one-third of the whipped cream into the chocolate mixture, then gently fold in the remaining whipped cream in two additions.

8. Strain the mixture through a fine-mesh sieve into a large bowl.

9. Spoon or pipe the mousse into 8 (⅓-cup) half-sphere molds, and then pipe mousse into 8 (1 x 4-inch) acetate tube molds. Transfer to the freezer until firm, 3 to 4 hours.

1. Soak the gelatin sheets in a small bowl of very cold water until softened, 15 minutes.

2. Melt the chocolate in a medium heatproof bowl over a saucepan of just-simmering water, stirring occasionally, over low heat, until smooth (do not let the bowl touch the water). Remove from the heat, stir in the vanilla, and set aside to cool slightly.

3. In a small saucepan over medium heat, stir together the sugar and water until the sugar dissolves. Attach a candy thermometer to the side of the saucepan, and continue to cook the sugar without stirring until the syrup reaches 243°F (118°C).

4. Meanwhile, in a medium bowl, use a handheld mixer to beat the egg yolks at high speed.

5. When the sugar syrup reaches the correct temperature, continue to beat the egg yolks while slowly pouring the syrup in a steady stream down the side of the bowl; make sure the syrup does not come in contact with the beaters. Continue to beat the mixture until it is almost white in color and it cools to a temperature of 85°F (29°C).

6. Whisk the melted chocolate mixture into the egg yolk mixture.

7. In a small bowl, use a handheld mixer to beat the egg white at high speed to stiff peaks.

8. Fold the egg white into the white chocolate mixture in three additions.

9. In a small saucepan, bring milk just to a boil (when small bubbles begin to form) over medium heat. Remove from the heat.

10. Squeeze out any excess water from the softened gelatin sheets. Add the sheets to the milk and stir to dissolve.

11. Pour the milk mixture through a fine-mesh sieve into the chocolate mixture. Stir to combine well.

12. In a stand mixer fitted with the whip attachment, beat the heavy cream at high speed to soft peaks, about 2 minutes.

13. Fold the whipped cream into the white chocolate mixture in three additions.

14. Strain the mousse through a fine-mesh sieve into a medium bowl.

15. Spoon or pipe the mousse into 8 (⅓-cup) half-sphere molds, then pipe mousse into 8 (1 x ½-inch) acetate tube molds. Transfer to the freezer and chill until firm, 3 to 4 hours.

16. While the mousse chills, prepare the strawberry-raspberry coulis and the chocolate sauce.

tre TO MAKE THE STRAWBERRY-RASPBERRY COULIS

1. Stir together the berries and sugar in a small bowl. Set aside to macerate for 20 minutes.

2. Transfer the berries to a small saucepan and stir in the orange juice and zest. Cook over low heat until the strawberries are soft, 5 to 7 minutes.

3. Transfer the berry mixture to a blender or food processor and purée.

4. Strain the mixture through a fine-mesh sieve into a small bowl. Stir in the rum and set aside to cool.

quattro TO MAKE THE CHOCOLATE SAUCE

1. Place the chocolate in a medium heatproof bowl.

2. In a small saucepan, heat the cream, sugar, and vanilla over medium-low heat, stirring constantly, until the sugar dissolves. Bring just to a boil, then remove from the heat.

3. Pour the cream mixture over the chocolate; make sure the chocolate is completely covered. Set aside for 2 minutes.

4. Add the rum. Using a flexible spatula, stir together the chocolate and cream, starting in the center of the bowl and working your way out to the edges, until well combined.

5. Stir in the butter and set aside to cool.

finale TO ASSEMBLE AND SERVE

1. Remove the half-spheres and tubes of dark chocolate and white chocolate mousse from the freezer. Remove the half-spheres from the molds and transfer to individual dessert plates.

2. Working with one tube at a time, use a sharp paring knife to cut a very small slice off each end of the tube to level it.

3. Unwrap the tubes and use a small offset spatula to carefully transfer one tube to the top of each half-sphere. Pair white chocolate tubes with dark chocolate half-spheres, and dark chocolate tubes with white chocolate half-spheres.

4. Carefully transfer the dessert plates to the refrigerator to defrost the mousse, 15 to 20 minutes.

5. Meanwhile, reheat the chocolate sauce over low heat.

6. Just before serving, garnish the dessert plates with chocolate sauce, strawberry-raspberry coulis, and fresh berries. Top each tube with a raspberry. Serve with biscotti or amaretti and *una tazza di espresso e un buon bicchierino di liquore*, or "a cup of espresso and good shot of liqueur."

Parfait con Mousse al Cioccolato Bianco e Composta di Mirtilli

SERVES 6 TO 8

White Chocolate Mousse with Blueberry Compote Parfait

This parfait has only two layers, but you can easily make it with four layers instead for a showier presentation. If you have any leftover blueberry compote, it can be stored in an airtight container in the refrigerator for up to four days. It's delicious over pancakes, French toast, cake, panna cotta, or ice cream.

uno COMPOSTA DI MIRTILLI (BLUEBERRY COMPOTE)

  3½ cups (490 g) fresh blueberries, divided

  ¼ cup plus 2 tablespoons (75 ml) water, divided

  2 tablespoons (28 g) superfine sugar

  1 tablespoon (20 g) honey

  1 teaspoon cornstarch

  2 teaspoons Meyer lemon juice

  grated zest of 1 Meyer lemon

  2 tablespoons (30 ml) peach schnapps

due MOUSSE AL CIOCCOLATO BIANCO (WHITE CHOCOLATE MOUSSE)

  3½ sheets (6 g) gold gelatin sheets

  12 ounces (340 g) good-quality white chocolate, finely chopped

  2½ cups (590 ml) heavy cream, divided

  1 teaspoon pure vanilla extract

finale ASSEMBLY

  White Chocolate Curls (see below)

HOW TO MAKE CHOCOLATE CURLS

Chocolate curls are simple to make and the perfect way to dress up desserts.

1. Place a 4-ounce chocolate bar on a sheet of parchment paper. Warm the bar of chocolate by microwaving on low for 5-second intervals until the chocolate just starts to soften slightly. Be careful, because it doesn't take too long for the chocolate to melt.
2. To create curls, run the blade of a vegetable peeler lengthwise across one edge of the chocolate bar. If the chocolate breaks, the bar is too cold; return to the microwave to reheat before continuing.
3. Use a wooden skewer to transfer the curls to a dish. Refrigerate until firm, about 10 minutes. Curls are easiest to work with when they are cold and firm.
4. Store leftover curls in an airtight container in the refrigerator for up to 1 month.

uno   TO MAKE THE BLUEBERRY COMPOTE

1. In a medium saucepan over medium heat, bring 2 cups of the blueberries, ¼ cup plus 1 tablespoon of the water, sugar, and honey to a simmer, stirring to dissolve the sugar, about 4 minutes.

2. Dissolve the cornstarch in the remaining 1 tablespoon water. Strain the mixture through a small fine-mesh sieve into the blueberry mixture. Stir to combine well, and continue simmering until slightly thickened, about 2 minutes.

3. Add the remaining blueberries and the lemon juice and zest. Cook for 1 minute longer.

4. Remove from the heat and stir in the peach schnapps.

5. Spoon the warm compote into 6 to 8 parfait glasses. Set aside, allowing the compote to cool completely. Once cooled, cover the individual parfait glasses with plastic wrap and refrigerate until cold.

due   TO MAKE THE WHITE CHOCOLATE MOUSSE

1. Soak the gelatin in a small bowl of very cold water until softened, about 15 minutes.

2. Melt the white chocolate in a heatproof bowl set over a saucepan of just-simmering water (do not let the bowl touch the water), stirring occasionally, over low heat. Remove from the heat and set aside to cool slightly.

3. To prepare an ice water bath, half fill a large bowl with ice and cover the ice with cold water.

4. In a small saucepan over medium heat, bring ¾ cup (180 ml) of the cream just to a boil. Remove from the heat.

5. Remove the gelatin sheets from the water, squeeze out any excess liquid, and add the gelatin to the cream, stirring to dissolve.

6. Strain the cream mixture through a fine-mesh sieve into the melted chocolate and stir to combine well. Stir in the vanilla.

7. Place the bowl in the ice water bath. Chill, stirring occasionally, until the mixture is thickened and falls in ribbons from a spoon, about 8 minutes.

8. In a stand mixer fitted with the whip attachment, beat the remaining 1¾ cups cream at medium speed to soft peaks.

9. Fold one-half of the whipped cream into the chocolate mixture, then fold in the remaining whipped cream.

10. Strain the mousse through a fine-mesh sieve into an airtight container, cover, and refrigerate for 1 hour.

finale TO ASSEMBLE

1. Transfer the mousse to large pastry bag fitted with large plain tip.

2. Remove the parfait glasses from the refrigerator, and pipe white chocolate mousse over the blueberry compote.

3. Cover the individual parfaits with plastic wrap and refrigerate to chill, about 2 hours.

4. Serve garnished with white chocolate curls.

White Chocolate Mousse with Blueberry Compote Parfait

Coppa di Crema al Caramello con Pralina di Nocciole

Butterscotch Cream with Hazelnut Praline

2½ cups (590 ml) heavy cream

½ cup (120 ml) whole milk

1 vanilla bean, split and seeded

¾ cup (150 g) dark brown sugar or muscovado sugar

¼ teaspoon salt

⅓ cup plus ½ tablespoon (70 g) demerara sugar

¼ cup (60 ml) water

8 large egg yolks

Pralinata di Nocciola (Hazelnut Praline) (page 21), for garnish

Sweetened Whipped Cream (page 13), for garnish (optional)

1. Preheat the oven to 300°F (150°C). Line a deep baking dish with a folded kitchen towel. Bring a teakettle of water almost to a boil.

2. Meanwhile, in a heavy medium saucepan over medium heat, bring the cream, milk, vanilla bean and seeds, brown or muscovado sugar, and salt to a boil, stirring constantly to dissolve the sugar. Remove from the heat and cover to keep warm.

3. In a heavy large saucepan, sprinkle the demerara sugar over the water in an even layer. Bring to a boil over medium heat, stirring constantly until the sugar dissolves. Continue cooking, without stirring, occasionally swirling the pan over the burner until it turns a light caramel color, 2 to 3 minutes. Use a pastry brush dipped in water to wash down any crystals that form on the sides of the pan as the sugar cooks. Remove from the heat.

4. Gradually add the warm cream mixture to the caramel (be careful—it will splatter and bubble up), whisking constantly until smooth and well combined. (If you can see any clumps of sugar, return to the heat and whisk until the sugar dissolves.)

5. Whisk the egg yolks in a large bowl until pale in color. Gradually, in a slow, steady stream, add the hot cream mixture to the egg yolks, whisking constantly until well combined.

6. Using a fine-mesh sieve, strain the mixture into an extra-large heatproof measuring cup. Skim off any foam with a spoon. Let stand for 15 minutes, allowing any air bubbles that may have formed to dissipate.

7. Divide the custard evenly among 8 (4-ounce) ovenproof baking cups. Seal each cup with a piece of tin foil to prevent a tough skin from forming.

8. Transfer the sealed baking cups to the prepared baking dish, spacing them a few inches apart (the cups should not touch each other). Open the oven door and pull out the middle rack halfway; transfer the baking dish to the rack. Carefully fill the baking dish with enough hot water to come halfway up the sides of the cups. Carefully push in the oven rack.

9. Bake until the custard is set around edges but jiggles slightly in the center when the baking dish is gently shaken, about 40 minutes.

10. Carefully remove the baking dish from oven. Using tongs, carefully remove the custard cups from the water bath. Discard the foil tops and transfer to a wire rack to cool completely. The custard will continue to set as it cools.

11. Once cooled, refrigerate until firm, 2 to 3 hours. Remove from the refrigerator, allow the custard to come to room temperature, and serve garnished with hazelnut praline and a dollop of whipped cream, if using.

Butterscotch Cream with Hazelnut Praline

Panna Cotta al Cocco e Vaniglia con Gelatina di Melagrana

Vanilla-Coconut Panna Cotta with Pomegranate Jelly

Panna cotta is the perfect dessert to serve when you're hosting a large gathering. It's simple yet elegant, versatile, and best of all, it can be made a day or two in advance of your event. This recipe can easily go from serving a party of six to a party of twenty-four by simply serving it in 2-ounce liqueur glasses rather than 8-ounce serving glasses. For a fun presentation, you can build the panna cotta in tilted layers (this works especially well with 2-ounce glasses). Place an egg carton on a small rimmed baking sheet and place each glass at an angle in an egg slot. Carefully pour panna cotta into the glasses, filling three-quarters full, and refrigerate to set. When set, remove the glasses from the egg carton and stand them upright on the baking sheet. Pour pomegranate jelly filling flush to top of panna cotta layer and return to the refrigerator to set the jelly. If you have the time, you could do a few layers alternating panna cotta and jelly, making sure each layer is set before adding the next.

uno PANNA COTTA AL COCCO E VANIGLIA (VANILLA-COCONUT PANNA COTTA)

    2 cups plus 2 tablespoons (500 ml) coconut milk

    1 cup (240 ml) heavy cream

    1 cup (240 ml) light cream

    1 cup (225 g) superfine sugar

    1 vanilla bean, split and seeded

    2 packages (14 g) unflavored powdered gelatin

    ¼ cup plus 2 tablespoons (90 ml) very cold water

due GELATINA DI MELAGRANA (POMEGRANATE JELLY)

    1 package (7 g) unflavored powdered gelatin

    ¼ cup (60 ml) boiling water

    2 cups (475 ml) pomegranate juice

    2 teaspoons superfine sugar

finale ASSEMBLY

    pomegranate seeds

uno TO MAKE THE PANNA COTTA

1. In a medium saucepan over medium heat, bring the coconut milk, heavy cream, light cream, sugar, and the vanilla bean and seeds just to a boil, stirring until the sugar is dissolved. Remove from the heat, cover, and allow the vanilla to infuse for 20 minutes.

2. Sprinkle the gelatin over the water in a small bowl. Set aside to bloom, 5 to 10 minutes.

3. Pass the coconut mixture through a fine-mesh sieve into a medium bowl (discard any solids).

4. Add the bloomed gelatin to the coconut mixture and whisk to dissolve completely.

5. Pass the mixture through a fine-mesh sieve into a pourable container.

6. Place 6 (8-ounce) serving glasses or cups on a rimmed baking sheet, and fill each glass three-quarters full with panna cotta. Refrigerate to set, about 3 hours.

due TO MAKE THE POMEGRANATE JELLY

1. In a medium heatproof bowl, stir together the gelatin and boiling water until the gelatin is dissolved.

2. Add the juice and sugar, and stir until well combined and the sugar is dissolved.

3. Pass the pomegranate mixture through a fine-mesh sieve into a pourable container. (If the mixture is hot to the touch, set aside to cool, stirring occasionally, until room temperature.)

4. Pour the jelly over the set panna cotta. Return to the refrigerator to set the jelly, about 3 hours.

finale TO SERVE

1. Serve garnished with fresh pomegranate seeds.

Vanilla-Coconut Panna Cotta
with Pomegranate Jelly

Soufflè di Nutella
Nutella Soufflé

MAKES 4 (6-OUNCE) SERVINGS OR 6 (4-OUNCE) SERVINGS

4 large eggs

3 tablespoons (43 g) unsalted butter, softened

finely grated chocolate or cocoa powder, for dusting

¾ cup plus 1½ tablespoons (9 ounces or 257 g) Nutella

pinch of salt

1 tablespoon Frangelico (hazelnut liqueur) (optional)

1 teaspoon pure vanilla extract

vanilla ice cream or Sweetened Whipped Cream (page 13), to serve (optional)

1. Separate the eggs, placing the yolks in large bowl and the whites in the bowl of a stand mixer. Cover the bowls with plastic wrap and allow the eggs to come to room temperature, about 30 minutes.

2. Preheat the oven to 375°F (190°C). Using a small pastry brush with even, upward strokes, butter each ramekin well with about half of the softened butter (this will help the soufflé rise). Refrigerate the ramekins for 5 minutes. Apply a second coat of softened butter (to ensure the soufflé doesn't stick to the ramekin). Dust each ramekin liberally with grated chocolate or cocoa powder, rolling and tilting each ramekin to ensure it is evenly coated. Tap out any excess chocolate.

3. In a large heatproof bowl set over a saucepan of just-simmering water (do not let the bowl touch the water), heat the Nutella over medium-low heat, stirring constantly until smooth and melted. Remove from the heat and set aside to cool slightly.

4. Meanwhile, in the stand mixer fitted with the whip attachment, whisk the eggs and salt at medium speed for 1 minute. Increase the mixer speed to high and beat until stiff peaks form, about 3 minutes.

5. In a large bowl, using a large balloon whisk, whisk the egg yolks and melted Nutella until well combined.

6. Whisk in the Frangelico and vanilla.

7. Stir 2 tablespoons of the egg whites into the Nutella mixture. Using a large flexible spatula, carefully fold in the remaining egg whites in three additions.

8. Spoon the mixture into the prepared ramekins, filling each three-quarters full. Press a small spoon into the mixture to fill any gaps. Spoon more of the mixture into the ramekins, filling right to the top. Tap each ramekin on the countertop to fill in the sides.

9. Working with one ramekin at a time, hold the ramekin over the bowl of the filling. With the other, use a large palette knife and push it across the top of the ramekin (away from you) so the filling is

flat, letting the excess fall into the bowl. Wipe away any splashes off the outside of each ramekin and also from the rim (otherwise the filling will burn while baking).

10. To prevent the soufflé from sticking to the top of the mold and to help it rise evenly, run your thumb around the rim of each soufflé, slightly inside the filling.

11. Arrange the dishes on a rimmed baking sheet and bake until the soufflés rise by about two-thirds of their original height, and the tops are set but jiggle when moved, 15 to 17 minutes.

12. Serve immediately with a dusting of grated chocolate and a scoop of vanilla ice cream or a dollop of sweetened whipped cream, if using.

Nutella Soufflé

Frozen and Fruit Desserts

Sorbetto al Lampone

Raspberry Sorbet

Sorbetto is a water-based Italian ice cream. It is light, refreshing and it serves as a non-fat or low-fat alternative to gelato. *Sorbetto* is often confused with granita but the textures are different. Granita has large size ice crystals giving it a crunchier texture whereas the texture of *sorbetto* is more like gelato, creamier. Enjoy *sorbetto* served in summer cocktails, floats, and fruit salad, with a few crunchy cookies like biscotti, or serve scooped in homemade *pizzelle* cups or cones (see page 93). It's also popular as a palate cleanser between the courses of a meal.

1 cup (240 ml) bottled or filtered water

1 cup (225 g) superfine sugar

4 cups (492 g) raspberries

1½ tablespoons freshly squeezed lemon juice

2 ounces (60 milliliters) vodka

1 large egg white

1. To make the sugar syrup, in a small saucepan over medium heat, bring the water and sugar to a boil, stirring to dissolve the sugar. Set aside to cool.

2. In a blender or food processor, process the raspberries and lemon juice to a smooth purée. Strain the purée through a fine-mesh sieve to remove the seeds (discard the solids).

3. Stir the purée into the cooled sugar syrup, and then stir in the vodka.

4. Transfer the mixture to a medium bowl, cover, and refrigerate until cold, at least 2 hours, or preferably overnight.

5. Immediately before churning the sorbet, use a handheld mixer to beat the egg white at high speed to stiff peaks. Fold the whipped egg white into the cooled raspberry mixture.

6. To ensure a seed-free or almost seed-free sorbet, strain the mixture again through a fine-mesh sieve into a pourable container.

7. Pour the raspberry mixture into an ice cream maker and process according to manufacturer's instructions. The sorbet will still be fairly soft but it will become firmer as it freezes.

8. Transfer the sorbet to an airtight container. Cover and freeze until firm, at least 2 hours.

9. To serve the sorbet at its best, remove from the freezer and transfer to the refrigerator 15 minutes before serving. Sorbet should be served slightly soft, with a creamy consistency similar to that of soft serve ice cream.

Sorbetto al Limone
Lemon Sorbet

Follow the preparation for Sorbetto al Lampone, but make the following modifications:

1. In Step 1, increase the filtered water to 1¾ cups plus 2½ tablespoons (450 ml) and increase the sugar to ¾ cup plus 2¼ tablespoons (200 g). Add the zest of 2 lemons. Use a vegetable peeler to cut long strips of zest with no pith (the white membrane).

2. In Step 2, replace the raspberries with the pulp and juice of 6 lemons (remove the seeds before blending). After blending and straining the lemon mixture, measure ¾ cup plus 1½ tablespoons (200 ml) juice (any leftover juice can be saved for other uses).

3. In Step 3, stir the measured lemon juice into the sugar syrup along with the vodka. Remove the lemon zest from the sugar syrup.

4. Proceed with the recipe instructions, beginning with Step 4 and skipping Step 6.

VARIATION *Sorbetto all'Arancia*
Orange Sorbet

Follow the preparation for Sorbetto al Lampone, but make the following modifications:

1. In Step 1, increase the filtered water to 2 cups (474 ml) and increase the sugar to ¾ cup plus 2¼ tablespoons (200 g). Add zest of 1 orange. Use a vegetable peeler to cut long strips of zest with no pith (the white membrane).

2. In Step 2, replace the raspberries with the pulp and juice of 5 oranges (remove the seeds before blending). After blending and straining the orange mixture, measure 1½ cups (350 ml) juice (any leftover juice can be saved for other uses).

3. In Step 3, stir the measured orange juice into the sugar syrup along with the vodka. Remove the orange zest from the sugar syrup

4. Proceed with the recipe instructions, beginning with Step 4 and skipping Step 6.

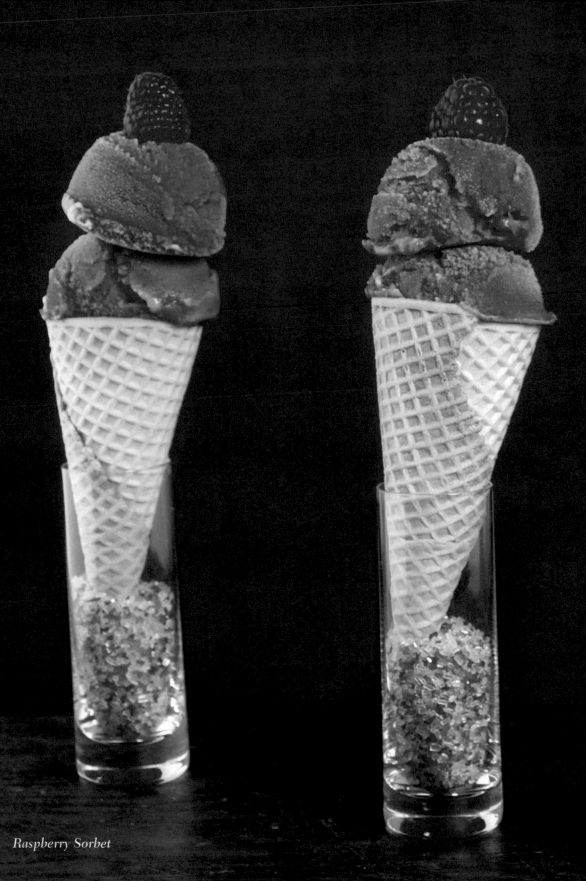

Raspberry Sorbet

Semifreddo alla Fragola, Vaniglia e Cioccolato

Strawberry, Vanilla, and Chocolate Semifreddo

Semifreddo, meaning "half cold," is an iced dessert, essentially a frozen mousse. Italians often refer to *semifreddo* as "parfait." Italian meringue and whipped cream are equally important components in a *semifreddo*, lightening the mixture and giving it a mousselike texture. They also prevent the *semifreddo* from freezing completely, which in turn enhances the creaminess. The basic Italian meringue recipe in this book makes more than you'll need for this *semifreddo*; the remaining meringue can be used to decorate the finished dessert.

After you prepare each layer of the *semifreddo* cover and refrigerate whipped cream. Cover meringue and set-aside at room temperature.

> 1¾ cups Pasta a Bomba (page 16)
>
> 2½ cups plus ½ tablespoon (600 ml) cold heavy cream, divided
>
> 1½ cups (216 g) strawberries, hulled and quartered
>
> 1 tablespoon superfine sugar
>
> 1 heaping cup (100 g) Meringa all'Italiana (Italian Meringue) (page 15)
>
> 1 vanilla bean, split and seeded
>
> 3½ ounces (100 g) good-quality semisweet chocolate, finely chopped
>
> fresh berries, for garnish

1. Line an 8½ x 4½ x 2½-inch loaf pan with parchment paper, leaving a 4-inch overhang on all 4 sides.

2. Divide the *pasta a bomba* equally among three separate bowls. Set aside, whisking occasionally to prevent a crust from forming.

3. Prepare the Italian meringue, cover, and set aside until ready to use. Also be sure to cover between preparing the layers of the *semifreddo*.

4. In a medium bowl, use a handheld mixer to beat 2 cups plus 2 tablespoons (500 ml) heavy cream at high speed to soft peaks. Refrigerate until ready to use. Also be sure to refrigerate between preparing the layers of the *semifreddo*.

5. In a blender, purée the strawberries and sugar. Press the purée through a fine-mesh sieve into one of the bowls of *pasta a bomba*. Stir until well combined. Fold in one-third of the Italian meringue, and then fold in one-third of the whipped cream in three additions.

6. Press the strawberry mixture through a fine-mesh sieve into the prepared loaf pan. Level, cover with plastic wrap, and freeze until firm, about 30 minutes.

7. Meanwhile, in a small saucepan, heat the cream and the vanilla bean and seeds until tiny bubbles start to form around the sides of the pan. Remove from the heat, cover, and allow to steep for 15 to 20 minutes.

8. Strain the vanilla cream through a fine-mesh sieve (discard the solids) and add to the second bowl of *pasta a bomba*. Stir until well combined. Fold in one-third of the Italian meringue, and then fold in one-third of the whipped cream in three additions.

9. Press the vanilla mixture through a fine-mesh sieve into the loaf pan over the firm strawberry layer. Level, cover with plastic wrap, and freeze until firm, about 30 minutes.

10. Before you begin making the chocolate layer, make sure the vanilla layer is firm. Then melt the chocolate in a heatproof bowl set over a pan of just-simmering water (do not let the bowl touch the water). Set aside to cool slightly.

11. Pour the melted chocolate into the remaining bowl of *pasta a bomba*, and stir until well combined. Don't be alarmed, this mixture will be quite thick. Fold in the remaining one-third of the Italian meringue, and then fold in the remaining one-third of the whipped cream in three additions.

12. Strain the chocolate cream through a fine-mesh sieve into the loaf pan over the firm vanilla layer. Level and cover with plastic wrap. Freeze for 4 hours or overnight.

13. Remove from the freezer 10 to 15 minutes before serving. Remove from the pan immediately (much easier when it is frozen) and transfer to a cake plate. Refrigerate or leave at room temperature to soften.

14. To serve, garnish with fresh berries. If you have any extra meringue, transfer it to a pastry bag fitted with a large tip and decorate the *semifreddo*.

Strawberry, Vanilla, and Chocolate Semifreddo

Fichi allo Zabaione

Figs with Zabaglione Cream

Zabaglione or *zabaione* is simple, delicate classic Italian liquid custard. It's usually served in a bowl accompanied by dry cookies or fresh fruit for dipping, or it's served over fruit with whipped cream. It's also used in a variety of desserts like tarts and tiramisu. It's traditionally prepared with egg yolks and sugar enriched with fortified wine like dry marsala, Madeira, or port. Traditional *zabaglione* is prepared with raw egg yolks, but today most people cook the custard in a bain-marie. The preparation for *zabaglione* is a simple one, but it's challenging to get it just right. *Zabaglione* should be light, fluffy, and flavorful. It's important to incorporate a lot of air into the mixture and to make sure the bowl does not get too hot, which risks scrambling the eggs.

Figs are a favorite in my family and only available locally for a few weeks out of the year. We eat a lot of figs in those few short weeks. One of our favorite ways to enjoy the figs is roasted with *zabaglione*. The flavors are exceptional.

> *24 Black Mission figs, halved*
>
> *6 large egg yolks, at room temperature*
>
> *½ cup plus ½ tablespoon (120 g) superfine sugar*
>
> *⅓ cup (80 ml) dry marsala*
>
> *demerara sugar, as needed*
>
> *¼ cup (28 g) walnuts, toasted and finely chopped, for garnish (see page 20)*
>
> *honey, for drizzling (optional)*

1. Evenly divide the fig halves among 6 ovenproof dishes (4 whole figs per dish). Place the dishes on a rimmed baking sheet and set aside.

2. In a small saucepan over medium heat, bring 2 inches of water to a boil.

3. In a large heatproof bowl, use a handheld mixer on high speed to beat the eggs and sugar until thick and pale in color (almost white) and the sugar is completely dissolved, about 5 minutes.

4. Reduce the mixer speed to low, and with the mixer running, add the marsala gradually in a thin stream, beating just to combine.

5. Place the bowl over the saucepan, making sure the bottom of the bowl is not touching the water. Reduce the heat to maintain a simmer (make sure the water doesn't boil). Beat the egg mixture at medium-high speed until thick and frothy, about 10 minutes. If the bowl gets too hot at any time, remove from heat allowing it to cool a bit but continue to beat off the heat. (If the bowl gets too hot, the eggs will scramble.)

6. Remove the bowl from the heat and set aside to cool slightly.

7. Position an oven rack as close to the broiler as possible and preheat the broiler.

8. Spoon the custard over top of the figs; sprinkle demerara sugar over the top and broil until the sugar caramelizes, 3 to 5 minutes. Watch the caramelization carefully; rotate the dishes if necessary to ensure the sugar doesn't burn.

9. Remove from the oven and serve warm with a drizzling of honey, if using, and a sprinkling of toasted walnuts.

Figs with Zabaglione Cream

Baked Peaches with Amaretti and Walnut Filling

Pesche al Forno con Ripieno D'Amaretti e Noce

SERVES 8 TO 12

Baked Peaches with Amaretti and Walnut Filling

4 large or 6 medium peaches

42 small amaretti cookies (120 g or 4½ ounces) crushed

¼ cup plus 2¼ teaspoons (56 g) golden cane sugar or turbinado sugar

1½ tablespoons (11 g) unsweetened cocoa, sifted

3 ounces (85 g) good-quality dark chocolate, finely chopped

¼ cup (28 g) walnuts, coarsely chopped

2 large egg yolks

½ teaspoon pure vanilla extract

1 to 2 tablespoons rum

1 tablespoon strong brewed coffee

¼ cup (56 g) unsalted butter

brown sugar, for sprinkling (optional)

mascarpone cheese, Sweetened Whipped Cream (page 13), or vanilla ice cream, to serve

1. Preheat the oven to 350°F (180°C). Butter the bottom of a large, shallow ovenproof dish.

2. Seal the amaretti cookies in a zip-top plastic bag and crush them finely with a rolling pin, or pulse in a food processor. Transfer the crushed cookies to a medium bowl. Stir in the sugar, cocoa, chocolate, and walnuts.

3. In a small bowl, beat the egg yolks, vanilla, rum, and coffee with a fork. Stir the egg mixture into the cookie mixture until well combined. (If the mixture is too wet, add a few more crushed amaretti cookies.)

4. Cut the peaches in half and remove the stones. Using a melon baller or spoon, carefully scoop out the flesh, in order to create a space for the filling. In a small bowl, mash the extra peach flesh with a fork and then add it to the filling. Stir to combine well.

5. Arrange the peaches cut-side up in the prepared dish. Divide the filling equally among the peaches and dot the top of each filled peach with the butter. If using brown sugar, sprinkle over the peaches. Bake until the peaches are tender but firm, 30 to 35 minutes.

6. Serve warm with mascarpone, sweetened whipped cream, or a scoop of vanilla ice cream.

FROZEN AND FRUIT DESSERTS *189*

Pesche al Vino Rosso

Peaches in Red Wine

When I was a child, we had several peach trees growing in our backyard. We frequently enjoyed *pesche al vino*, but it was a more casual, simpler version than this recipe. To make it the traditional way, and how my father prepared it for us, pit and slice ripe peaches. Place the slices in a wine glass and cover them with red or white wine. Allow to soak for 10 minutes, then lift the peaches from the wine and enjoy!

4 medium ripe peaches

¼ cup (50 g) brown sugar

2 cups plus 2 tablespoons (500 ml) fruity red wine such as Montepulciano D'Abbruzzo (about ⅔ of a 750 ml bottle)

1 cinnamon stick

3 strips lemon zest

½ vanilla bean, split and seeded

fresh raspberries, for garnish

fresh mint, for garnish

1. To peel the peaches, prepare an ice water bath; half fill a medium bowl with ice, and cover the ice with cold water. Bring a medium saucepan of water to a boil. Use a sharp paring knife to carve a very small cross-shaped incision in the bottom of each peach. Drop the peaches in the boiling water for about 1 minute. Remove with a spider skimmer or slotted spoon and plunge into the ice water. Carefully peel the skin off each peach and place in a medium, deep bowl.

2. Sprinkle half of the brown sugar over the peaches, then carefully turn them over and sprinkle with the remaining brown sugar. Set aside.

3. Combine the wine, cinnamon, lemon zest, and the vanilla bean and seeds in a small saucepan. Simmer over medium heat for 3 to 4 minutes.

4. Remove from the heat and pour the wine mixture over the peaches. Cover with a lid or plastic wrap and let stand at room temperature for 2 hours, turning the peaches occasionally to ensure even coloring as the peaches take on the color of the wine. (For even coloring, it is best to use a deep bowl so the peaches are completely immersed in the liquid. I also prepare a cartouche [see page 76] and weigh it down with a couple of spoons to keep the peaches from floating above the liquid. Be gentle so you don't bruise the peaches.)

5. Use a slotted spoon to transfer the peaches to an airtight container, being careful not to bruise them; cover and chill for 30 minutes.

6. Strain the wine mixture through a sieve and discard the solids. Chill until ready to serve.

7. To serve, place the peaches in shallow bowls and divide the spiced wine among the bowls. Garnish with fresh raspberries and a sprig of mint.

Crumble di Lamponi e Mirtilli con Pistacchio e Mandorle

Raspberry, Blueberry, and Pistachio-Almond Crumble

uno CRUMBLE AL PISTACCHIO E MANDORLE
(PISTACHIO-ALMOND CRUMBLE TOPPING)

1¼ cups (100 g) rolled oats

⅓ cup (50 g) raw pistachios, coarsely chopped

⅓ cup (40 g) slivered almonds, coarsely chopped

½ cup (100 g) light brown sugar

1 teaspoon ground cinnamon

pinch of salt

7 tablespoons (100 g) unsalted butter, at room temperature, cut into small pieces

due RIPIENO DI LAMPONI E MIRTILLI (RASPBERRY AND BLUEBERRY FILLING)

2 cups (246 g) raspberries

2 cups (296 g) blueberries

½ cup (113 g) superfine sugar

1 teaspoon pure vanilla extract

⅔ cup (160 ml) freshly squeezed orange juice (from about 2 medium oranges)

grated zest of 1 orange

pinch of salt

2 tablespoons (16 g) all-purpose flour

½ teaspoon cinnamon sugar

finale ASSEMBLY

vanilla ice cream or Sweetened Whipped Cream (page 13), to serve

uno TO MAKE THE PISTACHIO-ALMOND CRUMBLE TOPPING

1. In small bowl, stir together the oats, pistachios, almonds, brown sugar, cinnamon, and salt until well combined.

2. Rub the butter into the oat mixture with your fingertips until the butter is in pea-size pieces. Cover and refrigerate.

due TO MAKE THE RASPBERRY-BLUEBERRY FILLING

1. Preheat the oven to 350°F (180°C). Line a rimmed baking sheet with parchment paper. Butter 4 (6½-ounce) ovenproof dishes. Transfer to the baking sheet and set aside.

2. In a medium bowl, gently combine the raspberries, blueberries, superfine sugar, and vanilla extract until combined. Be careful not to crush the berries.

3. Add the orange juice and zest, and the salt. Sift the flour over the mixture and gently stir to just combine.

finale TO ASSEMBLE

1. Divide the filling evenly among the prepared dishes.

2. Sprinkle the cinnamon sugar on top of the filling, then evenly divide the pistachio-almond topping among the dishes.

3. Bake until the juices start to bubble and the topping is crisp and golden brown, 25 to 35 minutes.

4. Transfer the baking sheet to a wire rack and allow the crumbles to cool until warm. Serve warm with a scoop of vanilla ice cream or sweetened whipped cream.

Raspberry, Blueberry, and Pistachio-Almond Crumble

Vanilla Poached Pears

Pere al Vaniglia

Vanilla Poached Pears

Poached pears can be enjoyed on their own or served with panna cotta, cake, or ice cream.

2⅔ cups (630 ml) water

1¼ cups (240 g) demerara sugar

6 small pears (like Forelle), firm but ripe

1 vanilla bean, split and seeded

1 cinnamon stick

1. Make a cartouche from a piece of parchment paper (see page 76).

2. In a medium saucepan over medium heat, bring the water and sugar to a boil, stirring until the sugar is completely dissolved.

3. Meanwhile, peel the pears with a vegctable peeler, keeping as much of the pear's natural shape as possible. Cut the pears in half and core with a melon baller.

4. Reduce the heat to medium-low, and add the vanilla bean and seeds, and the cinnamon stick to the poaching liquid.

5. Add the prepared pears to the poaching liquid cored-side down. Cover the pears with the cartouche. Gently simmer, flipping the pears halfway through cooking time, until the pears are tender when pierced with a skewer, but still hold their shape, 15 to 25 minutes.

6. Remove from the heat and remove the cartouche. Allow the pears to cool in the poaching liquid.

7. If you would like to make use of the poaching liquid, remove the vanilla bean and cinnamon stick and then cook the liquid over medium-high heat until it reduces by half and becomes a thick syrup (keep an eye on the liquid—you don't want it to darken too much). Drizzle the warm syrup over warm pears and serve with ice cream.

8. Poached pears can be stored in an airtight container in the poaching liquid in the refrigerator for 3 or 4 days. Reheat and prepare the syrup, if using, prior to serving.

Recipe Index

Acknowledgments

To my talented daughter, Liana. A big thank you for the endless hours you've dedicated to shooting and editing all the photographs for my website, for the hours you've spent on the photos for this book, and for everything you do each and every day. And to my wonderful son, Matthew, better known as my "handsome dude," for the repeated trips up and down the stairs gathering my ingredients and tools, for washing dishes at 3 a.m., and for giving me a hug when things didn't go as planned. I love you both!

To my loving family, I thank you for helping me through my grief and sharing in my new journey. Each and every one of you has been significant in my healing. I'm surrounded with your love every day—what could be better than that? Thank you to my amazing sisters, Connie and Anna, for always being there for me. Your never-ending support makes me feel like I can do anything. And to my brothers, Luciano and Gabriel, I can't find the words to adequately thank you for the strength and inspiration you've given me. Special thank-yous to my cousins Ann-Marie and Jeanne. I love you all.

To my dearest friend Marly McMillen Beelman of NamelyMarley.com, for the day in and day out support, and most of all friendship. Thank you to Marly and Dennis, for your guidance and support, and helping me get my words to paper.

To everyone at Ulysses Press: Keith Riegert, acquisitions editor, for giving me this wonderful opportunity—it's given me a new lease on life; Lauren Harrison, my editor, for helping me come alive through the pages of this book; and to everyone behind the scenes. It's surreal that so many people worked together to bring my dreams to paper.

Thank you to the food blogging community and all the wonderful friends I've met online. Your inspiration makes me strive to improve every day. And a special thank you to all my readers—none of this would be possible without you; you've made sharing so easy.

And last, but definitely not least, to my parents, Vera and Ermando Massa. Papà, I know you're looking down on me, but I wish more than anything that you were here to share this wonderful time in my life. I miss you and love you—*Tanti abbracci e baci Papà*! And Mom, you're my inspiration and my strength. You've always believed I could accomplish whatever I set my mind to. I love you, Mom!

About the Author

Grace Massa Langlois was born in Maasmechelen, Belgium, to Italian parents Vera and Ermando Massa. She grew up in London, Ontario, where she lives with her two children, Liana and Matthew.

Backed by a business education, Grace began a career in finance at one of the largest banks in Canada. Her experience took her to the automotive industry as a financial services manager. She excelled in her field, but a debilitating injury forced an early retirement in 2003. Worse still, her husband, Maurice, suddenly passed away a short time later. With some encouragement from her children, Grace decided to share her love of good food, and in April 2010 launched her website, GracesSweetLife.com. Here, she shares recipes, stories about her Italian heritage, and the joy of growing up in a large, close-knit family. Liana is the face behind the camera, shooting all the photography. Matthew holds the difficult (but enviable) position of being the official taste tester.

Grace's recipes show her talent for making complicated desserts accessible to the everyday home cook. She strives to share her message that by learning the basics using fresh ingredients, home cooks can enjoy restaurant-style desserts at home.